Riddles of Existence

Riddles of Existence

A Guided Tour of Metaphysics

Earl Conee and Theodore Sider

CLARENDON PRESS · OXFORD

OXFORD
UNIVERSITY PRESS

Great Clarendon Street, Oxford OX2 6DP

Oxford University Press is a department of the University of Oxford.
It furthers the University's objective of excellence in research, scholarship,
and education by publishing worldwide in

Oxford New York

Auckland Cape Town Dar es Salaam Hong Kong Karachi
Kuala Lumpur Madrid Melbourne Mexico City Nairobi
New Delhi Shanghai Taipei Toronto

With offices in

Argentina Austria Brazil Chile Czech Republic France Greece
Guatemala Hungary Italy Japan Poland Portugal Singapore
South Korea Switzerland Thailand Turkey Ukraine Vietnam

Oxford is a registered trade mark of Oxford University Press
in the UK and in certain other countries

Published in the United States
by Oxford University Press Inc., New York

© Earl Conee and Theodore Sider 2005

British Library Cataloguing in Publication Data
Data available

Library of Congress Cataloging in Publication Data
Data available

Typeset by SPI Publisher Services, Pondicherry, India
Printed in Great Britain
on acid-free paper by
Biddles Ltd, King's Lynn, Norfolk

ISBN 0–19–928226–9   978–0–19–928226–5
1 3 5 7 9 10 8 6 4 2

CONTENTS

List of Figures   vii

Introduction   I
1. Personal Identity   7
2. Fatalism   22
3. Time   44
4. God   62
5. Why Not Nothing?   87
6. Free Will and Determinism   112
7. Constitution   134
8. Universals   154
9. Possibility and Necessity   181
10. What is Metaphysics?   197
Acknowledgments   207

Index   209

LIST OF FIGURES

1. The movement of a train defined by reference
   to time   45

2. The moving of the present moment   46

3. High-school physics graph of a particle moving
   through time   48

4. Space-time diagram   49

5. Where is the 'real here'?   51

6. 'Now' for me and for Guy Fawkes   52

7. Moving back and forth in space   55

8. Moving back and forth in time, temporal
   axis vertical   56

9. Moving back and forth in time, temporal
   axis horizontal   56

10. Four-dimensional perspective on the clay statue   148

11. David Lewis's actual and possible worlds   193

Introduction

You have a choice before you. Will you continue reading this book? Take your time, make up your mind ... OK, time's up. What is your decision?

If you have reached this sentence, your decision must have been *yes*. Now, think back to your decision. Was it a *free* decision? *Could* you have put the book down? Or did you *have* to keep reading?

Of course you could have put the book down; of course your decision was free. We human beings have free will.

Not so fast. We human beings are made of matter, tiny particles studied by the sciences. And the sciences, especially physics, discover laws of nature that specify where these particles must move. Given the forces that were acting on the particles, your body *had* to move the way it did, and so you had to continue to read. How then was your decision free?

This is the problem of free will. It is a tough problem. We all believe that we have free will, and yet scientific laws govern the matter making up our bodies, determining what we will do next. So do we have free will? Chapter 6 discusses this problem in depth, and suggests a certain answer. But it is not so important to us that you agree with our answer. What we really hope is that, by reading this book, you come to appreciate the importance of such problems and develop reasoned opinions of your own.

Grappling with the problem of free will, as with most other metaphysical issues, requires no specialized knowledge. The conflict between free will and science lies in what we already know. What philosophy teaches us is how to reflect on what we already know in a particularly careful and thoughtful way. It is truly astonishing what problems emerge from this kind of reflection!

The problem of free will is just one example of a metaphysical problem. Broadly and vaguely speaking, metaphysics addresses fundamental questions about the nature of reality. What are the basic ingredients of reality? What is their ultimate nature? Could reality have been different? And where do human beings fit into reality? Indeed, why does reality contain anything at all?

Philosophers at colleges and universities teach and write about metaphysics. They pursue deep questions about life, meaning, and the world. Bookstores also have large sections called Metaphysics or Metaphysical Studies, containing books on deep questions about life, meaning, and the world. But these books are rarely written by academic philosophers. Why is that?

The main reason is that what most philosophers write is too technical and specialized. That's a shame. Philosophy is exciting and important, and understandable by anyone. There may also be another reason. Academic philosophers try to be as rational as they can in their writings. They criticize each others' ideas ruthlessly in pursuit of the truth. This makes for controversies rather than soothing certainties, which some people don't like. But that's also a shame. The controversies are fun and enlightening. Philosophy is an intellectual quest, with rigorous rules designed to help us figure out what is really true.

Who's it For?

This book is for anyone interested in finding out about metaphysics. We take no background in philosophy for granted. The book is understandable without supplemental readings or instruction by a teacher.

As a textbook, it is flexible. The chapters are short and can be used independently of one another. The most accessible chapters come first; beyond that, the ordering has no great significance. In an introductory philosophy course, a section about metaphysics might use two or three chapters. A metaphysics course might use any or all of the chapters.

Who's it by?

It's by a couple of professors of philosophy. We each wrote five chapters. Though we collaborated on them all, we did not try to make the book read as if it were the work of one author. We hope that stylistic differences make for a pleasant and stimulating variation in tone.

What's it about?

The first nine chapters take up major topics in metaphysics; the last chapter considers the question of what metaphysics is. The chapters deal selectively with their issues. The goal is to take a serious look at these topics, without exhausting them—or the reader! A brief list of suggested further readings appears at the end of each chapter.

Chapter 1, Personal Identity (Sider)

Think back ten or twenty years into your past. You now have little in common with that earlier you. You look different. You think differently. And the matter now making you up is almost completely different. So why is that person *you*? What makes persons stay the same over time, despite such drastic changes?

Chapter 2, Fatalism (Conee)

Fatalism claims that everything is fated to be exactly as it is. Why believe that? Over the centuries, there have been intriguing arguments proposed in favor of it. We investigate how well these arguments work.

Chapter 3, Time (Sider)

Time can seem like the most mundane thing in the world, until you really start to think about it. Does time flow? If so, what could that mean? How fast does it flow, and can one travel back in time, against the current?

Chapter 4, God (Conee)

Does God exist? Yes, some say; and they claim to prove it. We examine some proposed proofs.

Chapter 5, Why Not Nothing? (Conee)

Why is there anything at all rather than nothing? Can we even understand this question? If so, what sort of answer might it have?

Chapter 6, Free Will and Determinism (Sider)

We all believe that we are free to act as we choose. But the business of science is to discover the underlying causes of things. Given science's excellent track record, it's a reasonable guess that it will one day discover the causes of human actions. But if our actions are caused by things that science can predict and control, how can we have free will?

Chapter 7, Constitution (Sider)

'If you hold a clay statue in your hand, you are actually holding *two* physical objects, a statue and a piece of clay. For if you squash the statue, the statue is destroyed but the piece of clay keeps on existing.' This argument seems to establish a very strange conclusion: two different objects can share exactly the same location. Can that be correct? If not, where did the argument go wrong?

Chapter 8, Universals (Conee)

Any two red apples have many things in common: most obviously, each is red and each is an apple. These things that they share, *redness* and *applehood*, are universals. Universals are very strange entities. For instance, redness seems to be in thousands of places at once: wherever any red object is located, redness itself is there. Do these universals really exist?

Chapter 9, Possibility and Necessity (Sider)

Not all truths are created equal. It is true that Michael Jordan is a great basketball player, and it is true that all bachelors are unmarried. Although each of these is a truth, there is a big difference between them. The first truth might have been false: Jordan might have decided never to play basketball. But the second truth could not have been false: bachelors are necessarily unmarried. What makes these truths so different?

Chapter 10, Metaphysics? (Conee)

After reading nine chapters about nine different metaphysical issues, you might expect to have a clear idea of what metaphysics is. But it is remarkably difficult to identify a unifying feature common to every metaphysical topic. We examine some ideas about the nature of metaphysics itself.

CHAPTER I

Personal Identity

Theodore Sider

The Concept of Personal Identity

On trial for murder, you decide to represent yourself. You are not
the murderer, you say; the murderer was a *different person* from
you. The judge asks for your evidence. Do you have photographs
of a mustachioed intruder? Don't your fingerprints match those
on the murder weapon? Can you show that the murderer is left-
handed? No, you say. Your defense is very different. Here are your
closing arguments:

I concede that the murderer is a righty, like me, has the same fingerprints
as I do, is clean-shaven like me. He even looks exactly like me in the
surveillance camera photographs introduced by the defense. No, I have
no twin. In fact, I admit that I remember committing the murder! But the
murderer is not the same person as me, for I have changed. That person's
favorite rock band was Led Zeppelin; I now prefer Todd Rundgren. That
person had an appendix, but I do not; mine was removed last week. That
person was 25 years old; I am 30. I am not the same person as that
murderer of five years ago. Therefore you cannot punish me, for no
one is guilty of a crime committed by *someone else*.

Obviously, no court of law would buy this argument. And
yet, what is wrong with it? When someone changes, whether

physically or psychologically, isn't it true that he's 'not the same person'?

Yes, but the phrase 'the same person' is ambiguous. There are two ways we can talk about one person's being the same as another. When a person has a religious conversion or shaves his head, he is *dissimilar* to how he was before. He does not remain **qualitatively** the same person, let us say. So in one sense he is not 'the same person'. But in another sense he *is* the same person: no other person has taken his place. This second kind of sameness is called **numerical** sameness, since it is the sort of sameness expressed by the equals sign in mathematical statements like '2+2=4': the expressions '2+2' and '4' stand for one and the same number. You are numerically the same person you were when you were a baby, although you are qualitatively very different. The closing arguments in the trial confuse the two kinds of sameness. You have indeed changed since the commission of the crime: you are qualitatively not the same. But you are numerically the same person as the murderer; no *other* person murdered the victim. It is true that 'no one can be punished for crimes committed by someone else'. But 'someone else' here means someone numerically distinct from you.

The concept of numerical sameness is important in human affairs. It affects whom we can punish, for it is unjust to punish anyone numerically distinct from the wrongdoer. It also plays a crucial role in emotions such as anticipation, regret, and remorse. You can't feel the same sort of regret or remorse for the mistakes of others that you can feel for your own mistakes. You can't anticipate the pleasures to be experienced by someone else, no matter how qualitatively similar to you that other person may be. The question of what makes persons numerically the same over time is known to philosophers as the question of **personal identity**.

The question of personal identity may be dramatized by an example. Imagine that you are very curious about what the future will be like. One day you catch God in a particularly good mood; she promises to bring you back to life five hundred years after your death, so that you can experience the future. At first you are understandably excited, but then you begin to wonder. How will God insure that it is *you* in the future? Five hundred years from now you will have died and your body will have rotted away. The matter now making you up will, by then, be scattered across the surface of the earth. God could easily create a new person out of new matter who resembles you, but that's no comfort. You want *yourself* to exist in the future; someone merely like you just won't cut it.

This example makes the problem of personal identity particularly vivid, but notice that the same issues are raised by ordinary change over time. Looking back at baby pictures, you say 'that was me'. But why? What makes that baby the same person as you, despite all the changes you have undergone in the intervening years?

(Philosophers also reflect on the identity over time of objects other than persons; they reflect on what makes an electron, tree, bicycle, or nation the same at one time as another. These objects raise many of the same questions that persons do, and some new ones as well. But persons are particularly fascinating. For one thing, only personal identity connects with emotions such as regret and anticipation. For another, *we* are persons. It is only natural that we take particular interest in ourselves.)

So how could God make it be *you* in the future? As noted, it is not enough to reconstitute, out of new matter, a person physically similar to you. That would be mere qualitative similarity. Would it help to use the same matter? God could gather all the protons, neutrons, and electrons that now constitute your body but will then be spread over the earth's surface, and form them into a person. For good measure, she could even make this new person look like you. But it wouldn't *be* you. It would be a new person made out of your old matter. If you don't agree, then consider this. Never mind the future; for all you know, the matter that now makes up your body once made up the body of another person thousands of years ago. It is incredibly unlikely, but nevertheless possible, that all the matter from some ancient Greek statesman has recycled through the biosphere and found its way into you. Clearly, that would not make you numerically identical to that statesman. You should not be punished for his crimes; you could not regret his misdeeds. Sameness of matter is not sufficient for personal identity.

Nor is it necessary. At least, *exact* sameness of matter isn't necessary for personal identity. People survive gradual changes in their matter all the time. They ingest and excrete, cut their hair and shed bits of skin, and sometimes have new skin or other matter grafted or implanted onto their bodies. In fact, normal processes of ingestion and excretion recycle nearly all of your matter every few years. Yet you're still you. Personal identity isn't especially tied to sameness of matter. So what *is* it tied to?

The Soul

Some philosophers and religious thinkers answer: the **soul**. A person's soul is her psychological essence, a nonphysical entity in which thoughts and feelings take place. The soul continues unscathed through all manner of physical change to the body, and can even survive the body's total destruction. Your soul is what makes you *you*. The baby in the pictures is *you* because the very same soul that now inhabits your body then inhabited that baby's body. So God can bring you back to life in the future by making a new body and inserting your soul into it.

Souls might seem to provide quick answers to many philosophical perplexities about identity over time, but there is no good reason to believe that they exist. Philosophers used to argue that souls must be posited in order to explain the existence of thoughts and feelings, since thoughts and feelings don't seem to be part of the physical body. But this argument is undermined by contemporary science. Human beings have long known that one part of the body—the brain—is especially connected to mentality. Even before contemporary neuroscience, head injuries were known to cause psychological damage. We now know how particular bits of the brain are connected with particular psychological effects. Although we are far from being able to completely correlate psychological states with brain states, we have made sufficient progress that the existence of such a correlation is a reasonable hypothesis. It is sensible to conclude that mentality itself resides in the brain, and that the soul does not exist. It's not that brain science *disproves* the soul; souls *could* exist even though brains and psychological states are perfectly correlated. But if the physical brain explains mentality on its own, there is no need to postulate souls in addition.

Also, soul theorists have a hard time explaining how souls manage to think. *Brain* theorists have the beginnings of an explanation: the brain contains billions of neurons, whose incredibly complex interactions produce thought. No one knows exactly how this works, but neuroscientists have at least made a good start. The soul theorist has nothing comparable to say, for most soul theorists think that the soul has no smaller parts. Souls are not made up of billions of little bitty soul-particles. (If they were, they would no longer provide quick answers to philosophical perplexities about identity over time. Soul theorists would face the same difficult philosophical questions the rest of us face. For instance: what makes a soul the same over time, despite changes to its soul-particles?) But if souls have no little bitty soul-particles, they have nothing like neurons to help them do their stuff. How, then, do they do it?

Spatiotemporal Continuity and the Case of the Prince and the Cobbler

Setting aside souls, let's turn to scientific theories, which base personal identity on natural phenomena. One such theory uses the concept of **spatiotemporal continuity**. Consider the identity over time of an inanimate object such as a baseball. A pitcher holds a baseball and starts his windup; moments later, a baseball is in the catcher's mitt. Are the baseballs the same? How will we decide? It is easiest if we have kept our eyes on the ball. A **continuous series**—a series of locations in space and time containing a baseball, the first in the pitcher's hand, later locations in the intervening places and times, and the final one in the catcher's mitt—convinces us that the catcher's baseball is the same as the pitcher's. If we observe no such continuous series, we may suspect that the baseballs are different. Now, we don't usually need this method to identify a person over time, since most people look very different from one another, but it could come in handy when dealing with identical twins. Want to know whether it is Billy Bob or Bobby Bill in the jail cell? First compile information from surveillance tape or informants. Then, using this information, trace a continuous series from the person in the jail backward in time, and see which twin it leads to.

Everyone agrees that spatiotemporal continuity is a good practical guide to personal identity. But as philosophers we want more. We want to discover the *essence* of personal identity; we want to know *what it is* to have personal identity, not merely how to tell when personal identity is present. If you want to know whether a man is a bachelor, checking to see whether his apartment is messy is a decent practical guide; if you want to tell whether a metal is gold, visual inspection and weighing on a scale will yield the right answer nine times out of ten. But having a messy apartment is not the *essence* of being a bachelor, for *some* bachelors are neat. Weighing a certain amount and appearing a certain way are not the essence of being gold, for it is possible for a metal to appear to be gold (in all superficial respects) but nevertheless not really *be* gold. (Think of fool's gold.) The true essence of being a bachelor is being an unmarried male; the true essence of being gold is having atomic number 79. For in no possible circumstance whatsoever is something a bachelor without being an unmarried man, and in no possible circumstance is something gold without having atomic number 79. All we require of practical guides for detecting bachelors or gold is that they work most of the time, but philosophical accounts of essence must work in all possible circumstances. The **spatiotemporal continuity theory** says that spatiotemporal continuity is indeed the essence of personal identity, not just that it is a good practical guide. Personal identity just *is* spatiotemporal continuity.

The theory must be refined a bit if it is really to work in every possible circumstance. Suppose you are captured, put into a pot, and melted into soup. Although we can trace a continuous series from you to the soup, the soup is not you. After being melted, you no longer exist; the matter that once composed you now composes something else. So we had better refine the spatiotemporal continuity theory to read as follows: persons are numerically identical if and only if they are spatiotemporally continuous via a series of *persons*. You are connected to the soup by a continuous series all right, but the later members of the series are portions of soup, not people.

Further refinements are possible (including saying that any change of matter in a continuous series must occur gradually, or saying that earlier members of such a series *cause* later members). But let's instead press on to a very interesting example introduced by the seventeenth-century British philosopher John Locke. A certain prince wonders what it would be like to live as a lowly cobbler. A cobbler reciprocally dreams of life as a prince. One day, they get their chance: *the entire psychologies of the prince and the cobbler are swapped*. The body of the cobbler comes to have all the memories, knowledge, and character traits of the prince, whose psychology has in turn departed for the cobbler's body. Locke himself spoke of souls: the souls of the prince and the cobbler are swapped. But let's change his story: suppose the swap occurs because the brains of the prince and the cobbler are altered, without any transfer of soul or matter, by an evil scientist. Although this is far-fetched, it is far from inconceivable. Science tells us that mental states depend on the arrangement of the brain's neurons. That arrangement could in principle be altered to become exactly like the arrangement of another brain.

After the swap, the person in the cobbler's body will remember having been a prince, and will remember the desire to try out life as a cobbler. He will say to himself: 'Finally, I have my chance!' He regards himself as being the prince, not the cobbler. And the person in the prince's body regards himself as being the cobbler, not the prince. Are they right?

The spatiotemporal continuity theory says that they are *not* right. Spatiotemporally continuous paths stick with *bodies*; they lead from the original prince to the person in the prince's body, and from the original cobbler to the person in the cobbler's body. So if the spatiotemporal continuity theory is correct, then the person in the cobbler's body is really the cobbler, not the prince, and the person in the prince's body is really the prince, not the cobbler.

Locke takes a different view; he agrees with the prince and the cobbler. If he is right, then his thought experiment refutes the spatiotemporal continuity theory. Here is a powerful argument on Locke's side. Suppose the prince had previously committed a horrible crime, knew that the mind-swap would occur, and hoped to use it to escape prosecution. After the swap, the crime is discovered, and the guards come to take the guilty one away. They know nothing of the swap, and so they haul off to jail the person in the prince's body, ignoring his protestations of innocence. The person in the cobbler's body (who considers himself the prince) remembers committing the crime and gloats over his narrow escape. This is a miscarriage of justice! The gloating person in the cobbler's body ought to be punished. If so, then the person in the cobbler's body *is* the prince, not the cobbler, for a person ought to be punished only for what he himself did.

Psychological Continuity and the Problem of Duplication

Locke took the example of the prince and the cobbler to show that personal identity follows a different kind of continuity, **psychological continuity**. According to the new theory that Locke proposed, the **psychological continuity theory**, a past person is numerically identical to the future person, if any, who has that past person's memories, character traits, and so on—whether or not the future and past persons are spatiotemporally continuous with each other. Locke's theory says that the gloating person in the cobbler's body is indeed the prince and is therefore guilty of the prince's crimes, since he is psychologically continuous with the prince. As we saw, this seems to be the correct verdict. But Locke faces the following fascinating challenge, presented by the twentieth-century British philosopher Bernard Williams.

Our evil scientist is at it again, and causes Charles, a person today, to have the psychology of Guy Fawkes, a man hung in 1606 for trying to blow up the English Parliament. Of course, it might be difficult to tell whether Charles is faking, but if he really does have Fawkes's psychology, then, Locke says, Charles *is* Guy Fawkes. So far, so good.

But now our scientist perversely causes this transformation *also* to happen to another person, Robert. Coming to have Fawkes's psychology is just an alteration to the brain; if it can happen to Charles, then it can happen to Robert as well. Locke's theory is now in trouble. Both Charles and Robert are psychologically continuous with Fawkes. If personal identity is psychological continuity, then both Charles and Robert would be identical to Fawkes. But that makes no sense, since it would imply that Charles and Robert are identical to each other! For if we know that

$$x = 4 \quad \text{and} \quad y = 4$$

then we can conclude that

$$x = y.$$

In just the same way, if we know that

$$\text{Charles} = \text{Fawkes} \quad \text{and} \quad \text{Robert} = \text{Fawkes}$$

then we can conclude that

$$\text{Charles} = \text{Robert}.$$

But it is absurd to claim that Charles = Robert. Though they are now qualitatively similar (each has Fawkes's memories and character traits), they are numerically two different people. This is the **duplication problem** for Locke's theory: what happens when psychological continuity is duplicated? (Or triplicated, or quadruplicated ...)

Williams chose spatiotemporal over psychological continuity because of the duplication problem. Before we follow him, let's think a little harder about spatiotemporal continuity. Just as a tree can survive the loss of a branch, a person can survive the loss of certain parts, even very large parts. You are still the same person if your legs or arms are amputated. Yet losing a part causes a certain amount of spatiotemporal discontinuity, since the region of space occupied by the person abruptly changes shape. Thus, 'spatiotemporal continuity' should be understood as meaning *sufficient* spatiotemporal continuity, in order to allow for change in parts while remaining the same thing or person.

How much continuity is 'sufficient' spatiotemporal continuity? Imagine that you have incurable cancer in the right half of your body but are healthy in the left. This cancer extends to your brain: the right hemisphere is cancerous while the left hemisphere is healthy. Fortunately, futuristic scientists can separate your body in two. They can even divide the brain's hemispheres and discard the cancerous half. You are given a prosthetic right arm and right leg, an artificial right half of your heart, and so on. You need no prosthetic right brain hemisphere, though, because the remaining healthy left hemisphere eventually functions exactly as your whole brain used to function. (Though fictional, this is not wholly far-fetched: the hemispheres of the human brain really can function independently when disconnected, and duplicate some—though not all—functions of each other.) Surely the person after the operation is the same as the person before: this operation is a way to save someone's life! But the operation results in a fairly severe spatiotemporal discontinuity, since the continuity between the person before and the person after is only the size of half the body. Moral: even the continuity of only half the body had better count as sufficient for personal identity.

But now the spatiotemporal continuity theory faces its own duplication problem. Let us alter the story of the previous paragraph so that the cancer is only in your brain, but is present in both hemispheres. Radiation treatment is the only cure, but it has a mere 10 percent chance of success. These odds are not good. Fortunately, they can be improved. Before the radiation treatment, the doctors divide your body—including the hemispheres—in two. Each half-body gets artificially completed as before; then the radiation treatment of the cancerous brain-halves begins. This gives you two 10 percent chances of success rather than one. But now comes the twist in the story: suppose the unlikely outcome is that *each* hemisphere gets cured by the treatment. So the operation results in two persons, each with one of your original hemispheres. Note that each is 'sufficiently' spatiotemporally continuous with you, since we agreed that a half-person's worth of continuity counts as sufficient. The spatiotemporal continuity theory then implies that you are identical to each of these two new persons, and we again have the absurd consequence that these two new persons are identical to each other.

Each of our theories, Locke's psychological continuity theory and the spatiotemporal continuity theory, faces the duplication problem. A single *original person* can be *continuous*, whether psychologically or spatiotemporally, with two *successor persons*. Each theory says that personal identity is continuity of some kind. So the original person is identical to each successor person, which then implies the absurdity that the successor persons are identical to each other. How should we solve this problem?

Some will be tempted to give up on scientific theories and instead appeal to souls. Continuity, whether psychological or spatiotemporal, does not determine what happens to a soul. When a body is duplicated, the soul in the original body might be inherited by one of the successor bodies, or by the other, or perhaps by neither, but not by both. While this is a tidy solution, it is unsupported by the evidence: there still is no reason to believe that souls exist. It would be better to somehow revise the scientific theories to take the duplication problem into account. (If we succeed, we will still need to decide between psychological and spatiotemporal continuity, or some combination of the two. But set this aside for the remainder of the chapter.)

As we originally stated the scientific theories, they said that personal identity is continuity. We could restate them to say instead that personal identity is **nonbranching** continuity. Continuity does not *normally* branch: usually only one person at a time is continuous with a given earlier person. In such cases there is personal identity. But the duplication examples involve branching, that is, two persons at a time who are both continuous with a single earlier person. So according to the restated theory, there is no personal identity in such cases. Neither Charles nor Robert is identical to Guy Fawkes. You do not survive the double-transplant operation.

Unlike the claim that the successor persons are identical to each other, this is not absurd. But it is pretty hard to accept. Imagine that, before the operation, you receive some good news: the left-hemisphere person will survive the division operation. Excellent. But now, if the modified spatiotemporal continuity theory is correct, then if the right-hemisphere person survives in addition, you will not survive. So it is *worse* for you if the right-hemisphere person survives. You must hope and pray that the right-hemisphere person will die. How strange! The news that the left-hemisphere person would survive was good; news that the right-hemisphere person would also survive just seems like more good news. How could an additional piece of good news make things much, much *worse*?

Radical Solutions to the Problem of Duplication

Duplication is a really knotty problem! Perhaps it is time to investigate some radical solutions. Here are two.

Derek Parfit, the contemporary British philosopher, challenges a fundamental assumption about personal identity that we have been making, the assumption that personal identity is *important*. Earlier in this chapter we assumed that personal identity connects with anticipation, regret, and punishment. This is part of the importance of personal identity. The last paragraph of the previous section assumed another part: that it is very bad for you if no one in the future is identical to you. That is, it is very bad to stop existing. Parfit challenges this assumption that identity is important. What is really important, Parfit says, is psychological continuity. In most ordinary cases, psychological continuity and personal identity go hand in hand. That is because, according to Parfit, personal identity is nonbranching continuity, and continuity rarely branches. But in the duplication case it does branch. In that case, then, you cease to exist. But *in the duplication case*, Parfit says, ceasing to exist is not bad. For even though you yourself will not continue to exist, you will still have all that matters: you will have psychological continuity (a double helping, in fact!).

Parfit's views are interesting and challenging. But can we really believe that utterly ceasing to exist is sometimes insignificant? That would require a radical revision of our ordinary beliefs. Are there other options?

We could instead reconsider one of our other assumptions about personal identity. The duplication argument assumes that if personal identity holds between the original person and each successor person, we get the absurd result that the successor persons are the same person as each other. But this absurd result follows only if personal identity is numerical identity, the same notion that the equals sign ($=$) expresses in mathematics. We made this assumption at the outset, but perhaps it is a mistake. Perhaps 'personal identity' is *never* really numerical identity. Perhaps all change *really does* result in a numerically distinct person. If so, then we would not need to say that branching destroys personal identity. For we could go back to saying that personal 'identity' is continuity (whether psychological or spatiotemporal—that remains to be decided). In branching cases, a single person can stand in the relationship of 'personal identity' to two distinct persons; that is not absurd if personal identity is not numerical identity. We would still need to distinguish mere qualitative similarity ('he's not the same person he was before going to college') from a stricter notion of personal 'identity' that connects with punishment, anticipation, and regret. But even this stricter notion would be looser than numerical identity.

Can we really believe that our baby pictures are of people numerically distinct from us? That too would require radical belief revision. But sometimes, philosophy calls for just that.

FURTHER READING

John Perry's anthology *Personal Identity* (University of California Press, 1975), is an excellent source for more readings on personal identity. It contains a selection from John Locke defending the psychological continuity view, a paper by Derek Parfit arguing that personal identity is not as significant as we normally take it to be, a paper by Thomas Nagel on brain bisection, and many other interesting papers. Perry's introduction to the anthology is also excellent.

Another good book, also called *Personal Identity*, is co-authored by Sydney Shoemaker and Richard Swinburne (Blackwell, 1984). The first half, written by Swinburne, defends the soul theory of personal identity, and is especially accessible. The second half, written by Shoemaker, defends the psychological continuity view.

Bernard Williams introduces the problem of duplication in 'Personal Identity and Individuation', in his book *Problems of the Self* (Cambridge University Press, 1973).

CHAPTER 2

Fatalism

Earl Conee

Introduction

Open possibilities are open to choice or chance. This status matters to us. We are hopeful about the positive possibilities. We worry about the threatening ones. We take an open possibility to be unsettled, up-in-the-air.

In contrast, fated things are out of anyone's control, bound to be. This status matters differently to us. If something fated looks bad, we try to resign ourselves to it. If something fated looks good, we are glad about it. We take anything fated to be a given.

Some philosophers have tried to prove that all of reality—everything that ever happens, every entity that ever exists, and every condition that things are ever in—all was forever fated to be as it is. This is the doctrine of **metaphysical fatalism**.

There are several things to set aside right away, because metaphysical fatalism does not say or imply that they are true. First, metaphysical fatalism is not about being fated by the Fates. The Fates are three ancient Greek mythical goddesses who were believed to decide human destiny. No philosopher thinks that those goddesses exist and determine our lives. Philosophers agree that nothing is fated by the Fates.

Metaphysical fatalism says that there is a kind of necessity to every actual thing. This does not imply that 'everything happens for a reason'. Metaphysical fatalism is about an impersonal necessity, not a reason or purpose. Also, metaphysical fatalism does not imply that we have a destiny where certain things would have to happen to us, no matter what else was to happen. Rather, it implies that our fate is to be exactly as we are, in exactly the situations that we are actually in. Furthermore, this fatalism does *not* imply that effort is futile. It allows that some efforts cause improvements—although it does imply that both the efforts and the resulting improvements were fated. Fatalists acknowledge that we do not always *know* what is going to happen. They say that it is all fated, regardless of what anyone knows about what will be.

Moreover, metaphysical fatalism does not tell us to be 'fatalistic', that is, to regard the future with resignation or submission to fate. No particular attitude is automatically justified. Fatalism even allows a cheerful optimism to be justified—maybe things are fated to go well and attitudes of resignation and submission do no good.

Finally, the necessity that metaphysical fatalists attribute to everything is not the necessity of causes to produce their effects. Clearly, many things are determined in advance by physical laws and prior conditions. If everything that ever happens is determined in this way, then what philosophers call **determinism** is true.[1] The melting of some ice that is heated above water's freezing point is inevitable. This seems enough to say that the heating makes the melting 'fated' to occur. But the truth of determinism would not be even partial support for metaphysical fatalism. Fatalism is not about being physically or causally determined. It is about something more abstract, something that does not depend on how things go in nature. Determinists hold that the present and future are causally determined by the past and the physical laws, but there could have been a different past or

[1] For more about determinism, see 'Free Will and Determinism', Chapter 6.

different laws. The metaphysical fatalists' view is that, even if determinism is not true, there are no open possibilities at any point in history. Their claim is that each thing in the past, present, and future has always been fixed and settled, whether or not it was causally determined.

Metaphysical fatalists think that the sheer presence of anything in the world gives the thing a necessity. Why? Fatalists present **arguments**—lines of reasoning—to try to prove their thesis. Let's look at some main fatalist arguments and see how well they work.

The Sea Battle

The ancient Greek philosopher Aristotle gives us our first argument. Here is a short story about some predictions.

> A sea battle may well take place tomorrow. Today, someone predicts that it will happen tomorrow and someone else predicts that it won't. Neither of the predictors knows what is going to happen. They are both just guessing.

That is the whole story. It is not a work of art. But our Aristotelian fatalist uses it to argue for something profound.

The Sea Battle argument begins as follows.

> *First Assumption*: Either the prediction that the battle will happen is true, or the prediction that it won't happen is true.

This First Assumption seems sensible, although it will not go unchallenged. Let's continue with the reasoning.

> *Second Assumption*: If a statement is true, then it has to be true.

This too initially seems right, though again we'll think more about it. From these two assumptions the fatalist derives the following.

Initial Conclusion: Whichever prediction about the battle is true, it has to be true.

If a prediction *has to be* true, then it describes a necessary fact. So now the fatalist derives this.

Second Conclusion: Whether or not a battle will take place at sea tomorrow, whichever will happen is something that has to be—it is necessary.

This conclusion is fatalistic. And there is more to come. So far, the Sea Battle argument is just about one predicted event. Metaphysical fatalism is about everything. A conclusion about everything can be reached by generalizing from the reasoning about the sea battle. Nothing in the story makes its battle especially prone to having the status of being settled in advance. So, to the extent that the argument about the battle succeeds, an unrestricted conclusion about everything else seems to be equally well supported.

One less-than-universal aspect of the story is that predictions have been made. That seems not to be crucial, though. The argument does not use the predicting as a basis for inferring the necessity of what is predicted. If the argument succeeds, then it would be *the reality of the situation* that makes the predicted fact necessary, not the predicting of it. Thus, the whole truth about the future would be necessary, whether predicted or not. So it looks as though, if the fatalist succeeds in proving the Second Conclusion, then there is no real further obstacle to proving the following.

General Fatalistic Conclusion: Whatever will be, has to be.

Before evaluating the Sea Battle argument, we should note two further things about it. First, battling involves choice. Frequently, fatalism is regarded as being about our having freedom of choice. Choice is an important focus for fatalistic arguments, because choices are some of our favorite examples of open possibilities.

We think that there are free choices that really could have gone either way.[2] But the fatalists' conclusion is not limited to excluding freedom of choice. The General Fatalistic Conclusion asserts that the whole future is necessary. If this conclusion is right, then it applies as well to the things that are supposed to be matters of chance according to science. For instance, according to contemporary physics, the time of the radioactive decay of a uranium atom is not physically determined. Two uranium atoms can be in exactly the same physical condition until one decays and the other does not. Yet the Sea Battle sort of argument applies here just as well. Consider two predictive statements made before noon, one saying that some particular uranium atom will decay at noon and the other denying that the atom will decay at noon. The rest of the Sea Battle argument transfers over to the example. We get the fatalistic conclusion that the state of the atom at noon, whether decayed or not, has to be.

The General Fatalistic Conclusion is only about the future. Full-blown metaphysical fatalism is about everything, past, present, and future. This is not an obstacle to fatalism, though. The Sea Battle argument reaching the General Fatalistic Conclusion about the future does all of the hard work. The past and present are easy for the fatalist to deal with. It is quite plausible that the past is just as the fatalist says it is—the whole past is fixed and settled. The same goes for the present. If anything is in some condition at present, then the thing's current condition is fixed and settled. The present is too late to do anything about the present!

Thus, past and present look ripe for fatalism. If the Sea Battle argument shows that the future is fixed and settled too, then the way seems clear for a final comprehensive fatalist conclusion: there are no open possibilities at all at any time.

[2] 'Free Will and Determinism', chapter 6, is about this.

Arguments rely on their assumptions. If an argument has a premise that is obviously untrue, then the argument is definitely a failure. Arguments that are taken seriously in metaphysics are seldom that bad. If one strikes us that way, we should strongly suspect that we have not understood it. Arguments can fail less conclusively, though. Another thing that keeps an argument from proving its conclusion is the existence of an unresolved doubt about a premise. Raising doubts about premises is how the Sea Battle argument is most often faulted. Let's see how well the premises stand scrutiny.

Some philosophers have objected to the Sea Battle argument's First Assumption, the premise saying that one of the two predictions about the battle is true in advance. This assumption is one version of a principle known as the **Law of the Excluded Middle** (LEM). Our version excludes any middle ground between the truth of a statement and the truth of its denial.

> LEM. Concerning any statement, either it is true or its denial is true.

At least at first, LEM appears irresistible. How could a statement be untrue while the statement denying that it was true—its denial—was untrue too? That would seem to require an unfathomable 'reality gap'—an intermediate condition between being and not being. And this could not be like a ghostly haze, since a ghostly haze is a way of being! Yet some philosophers have opposed the Sea Battle argument by arguing against LEM. They have contended that LEM applies only to statements that assert *settled* facts, such as statements about what has already happened. The critics say that other statements, like ones about a potential sea battle that may or may not take place, have no truth yet. The prediction that the battle will occur is not now true, and neither is its denial, because nothing that exists right now makes either one true. Both predictions are presently indeterminate rather than true. The critics conclude that LEM is false.

This criticism has a serious drawback. Suppose that Alice predicted yesterday, 'There will be a thunderstorm in Cleveland tomorrow', and in fact there is a thunderstorm in Cleveland today. It is only natural to think that Alice got it right *yesterday*. This means that what Alice said was already true when she said it. Maybe at the time no one *knew* whether or not it was true. Maybe at the time its truth was *unsettled*. Still, when we do find out about the storm today, we say that her prediction *was* correct. If so, then the prediction was not indeterminate yesterday after all. This seems to apply to predictive statements quite generally. If the future bears them out, then we regard what they say of the future as having been true when they were still predictions. The objection to the LEM denies that they were true in advance. So the objection is in trouble.

An opponent of LEM might be unimpressed. An opponent might first repeat the point that when a predicted event is not now a settled fact, there is nothing around now to *make* the prediction true. The opponent could then add that any statement is true only if something makes it true. Conceding that people *regard* these predictions as having been true when made, the opponent might insist that this need for a truth-maker shows that the predictions couldn't have *been* true in advance. This restores the conclusion that LEM is wrong about them.

Though this criticism is reasonable, there is a good reply. The reply is that, because predictions are *about* the future, what makes them true or untrue is *in* the future, not in the present. There does not have to be anything around *now* to make them true. In fact, now is too early. So long as things turn out in the future as predicted, then the predictions are made true now by those later developments. The truth-makers for accurate predictions are in the future, right where they belong.

LEM is looking difficult to refute. Other critics of the Sea Battle argument focus on its Second Assumption: if any statement is true, then it has to be true. The classic objection to this assumption begins by observing that the assumption has more than one meaning. The critics say that on the interpretation of its meaning where the assumption is correct, it does not help the argument. On the interpretation where it helps, it is not correct. Specifically, the assumption is correct if it means this.

SA1: It has to be that if a statement is true, then the statement is true.

SA1 is impeccable. But it says only that the following conditional claim has to be correct: if a statement is true, then it is true. This conditional claim is truly trivial. It says only that a statement *is* true if it's true. SA1 does not tell us that any statement *has to be* true if it's true. Compare: If a wall is red, then it's red. That is a necessary fact. It applies to all walls, including a formerly brown wall that was just painted red. Yet it surely does not tell us that the wall *has to be* red. Of course the wall doesn't have to be red— it was recently brown!

Likewise, the conditional claim—a statement is true if it's true—asserts a necessary fact. But it does not tell us that being *true* is all it takes for a statement to *have to be* true. Yet that is precisely what the Sea Battle needs to derive its conclusion—it needs true statements thereby *having to be* true. Looking back at the reasoning, we see that the argument uses the Second Assumption to draw the initial conclusion that there are predictions that *have to be* true. If any assumption brings into the argument this necessity for predictions, it is the Second Assumption, the one that we are now interpreting as SA1. Since SA1 does not bring in any such necessity, the argument's initial conclusion just does not follow logically if the argument uses SA1.

The Sea Battle argument does get what it needs for its initial conclusion to follow logically if the following interpretation of the Second Assumption is part of the argument.

> SA2: If a statement is true, then that statement has to be true.

SA2 does say that being true is enough for a statement to be necessary. So SA2 asserts the necessity of true predictions that the Sea Battle argument needs. But why believe SA2? To all appearances, some truths are **contingent**, that is, they are actually true but they need not have been true. We think that any lucky guess about something in the future that is not now settled is actually true, but not necessary. The truth of the guess derives from the occurrence later of what was guessed to happen. Yet SA2 says that even those lucky guesses about the apparently unsettled future would state necessary facts. SA2 says that just being true is enough to make any truth have to be true.

For us to find SA2 credible, we would have to find something about just being true that brings with it necessary truth. Nothing comes to mind. Being true by itself seems to allow that some things just happen to be true. The only temptation to think otherwise is a deception. We can be deceived by confusing SA2 with SA1. When we keep our minds clear of that confusion, though, SA2 is not reasonable to believe. Thus, either way we interpret the Second Assumption in the Sea Battle argument, the argument looks flawed at that point.

Past Predictions

The Sea Battle argument tries to use present truth to secure future necessity. We have seen that present truths may instead be secured by how the future happens to turn out. But what if something in the *past* guaranteed a specific future? After all, we are confident that once things are in the past, they are unalterable. So if the past secures the future, then the future is now necessitated.

Metaphysical fatalism has been defended on the basis of the claim that the truth about everything, including the future, already *existed* in the past. By virtue of existing in the past, this comprehensive truth is a fixed fact. This status of being settled in virtue of being past is sometimes called **accidental necessity**. The word 'accidental' here signifies that the fixity of the past is not absolutely necessary. There might have been a wholly different past instead. But once things are in the actual past, they do seem fixed and settled. So this is an 'accidental' sort of necessity. We think that the future is not likewise settled, at least not all of it. Choices and chance developments seem open, with some potential to develop in different ways. The Past Predictions argument seeks to show that the accidental necessity of the past carries over to the whole future.

A bit of philosophical terminology will be useful. The substance of a statement is what philosophers call a **proposition**. A proposition is what is said in a statement; it is the thought behind the words. Translations of the statement into another language aim to capture the same proposition in other words. Propositions are what we believe and otherwise think about when truth is at stake. If I predict that many good deeds will be done tomorrow, then the prediction is the proposition that many good deeds will be done tomorrow. If you hope that many good deeds will be done tomorrow, then this hope of yours has as its content the same proposition as my prediction.

These are propositions, *if* there really are any such entities. The existence of propositions is controversial among philosophers (as is the existence of everything else!) In any case, with the term 'proposition' understood in this way we are ready for the Past Predictions argument.

> *First Assumption*: For any way that things will be in the future, there existed in the past a true proposition to the effect that things would be that way.

The first assumption is about propositions that are contents of *available* predictions. It is not limited to the predictions that anyone has actually made. It says that the contents of all available true predictions existed in the past, whether or not anyone ever stated the predictions by asserting the propositions. The assumption says that an accurate prediction was always there to be made.

The First Assumption will be critically discussed soon.

> *Second Assumption*: Every aspect of the past is accidentally necessary.

This Second Assumption needs investigating. Clearly, everything we ordinarily regard as being in the past is fixed and settled— accidentally necessary. The second assumption goes beyond that, though, to claim that every last detail of the past of any sort is accidentally necessary. We'll look into that.

> *Preliminary Fatalistic Conclusion*: The truth in the past of each true predictive proposition is accidentally necessary.

If the truth of predictive propositions about everything in the future is accidentally necessary, then that locks in the whole future. So we have arrived at this.

> *General Fatalistic Conclusion*: the future in every detail is accidentally necessary.

Both assumptions of the Past Predictions argument are questionable. It is easy to have doubts about the existence of the countless unstated propositions that are required by the First Assumption. Does everything about the future correspond to some predictive proposition that *existed* in the past? Certainly, almost none of those predictions is ever actually *made* by anyone. Why think that the unstated predictive propositions exist?

An adequate investigation of the existence of propositions would take an extensive metaphysical inquiry. Though it would be terrifically interesting, it would be a very long digression here. Fortunately, we need not investigate this in order to appreciate the core of the Past Predictions reasoning. The argument would reach an impressive fatalistic conclusion even if it were scaled back to actual predictions so as to avoid this issue. People have actually predicted the sorts of things that we think remain open to future resolution. Some predictions have been made about apparently open choices. People have managed to predict—if only by luck—what someone later chose with all apparent freedom. Some accurate predictions have been made about other apparently open possibilities, such as the radioactive decay of a particle. The rest of the Past Predictions argument tells us that at least the actually predicted future outcomes have the accidental necessity of the corresponding true predictions. That is a fatalistic enough result to be remarkable. Predicted outcomes of these kinds seem to remain open just as much as ones that aren't predicted by anyone. This scaled back version of the argument skips the whole question of the existence of unstated truths. So let's restrict our thinking to actual predictions and proceed.

The Second Assumption of the Past Predictions argument is that every aspect of the past is accidentally necessary. True? When we consider the past, we tend to think of things that are *wholly* in the past: major historical events, our own previous adventures, and other things that are clearly purely in the past. Those are settled aspects of the past. Thinking of them makes the Second Assumption seem right. But what is crucial for the argument is whether certain *other* aspects of the past are in the same boat—the past truth of each true predictive statement.

The predictions have been made. So the past *existence* of the predictions is settled. A prediction's *truth*, though, is not something that is entirely accounted for by the past. A prediction is about the future. Because of this, if the prediction is true, then future circumstances are what make it true. This is just another way to say that things in the future settle the truth of the prediction. So, as long as some future things are currently unsettled, the truth of their past prediction is unsettled as well. It is reasonable for us to believe that some of the future remains open. We have just seen that, if this is so, then the truth of predictions about those aspects of the future remains unsettled too. Thus, it now looks as though the Past Predictions argument runs into trouble that is fundamentally the same as the problem for the Sea Battle argument. The problem arises here as the dubious assumption that every aspect of the past is accidentally necessary merely because it is in the past.

Necessary Conditions

I cannot finish off a mile-long run right now. Why? Because I need to have run almost a mile just before now, so that I can complete the running of a mile. Yet I have not been running. So I cannot finish a mile run at this point.

This explanation seems to say that there is a certain necessary condition for my finishing a mile run—my having run almost a mile—and the absence of this condition renders me unable to complete a mile run. The first assumption of our next fatalistic argument says that, quite generally, the absence of a necessary condition for an alternative always closes off the possibility of that alternative.

> *First Assumption*: Something is fixed and unalterable if any necessary condition for not having the thing is absent. (Restated in more positive terms: If something has an open alternative, then all that is needed for the alternative to exist is present.)

This First Assumption merits careful consideration. We'll investigate it after seeing the rest of the reasoning. The other assumption in the Necessary Conditions argument is rationally irresistible. It just says that any condition is needed in order to have that very condition.

> *Second Assumption*: Any condition is a necessary condition for itself.

To appreciate how these two assumptions work together to rule out any open alternatives, let's think about an example. Suppose that Cathy is about to make a choice between accepting a job offer and not accepting it. Suppose that Cathy will choose to accept the offer. Could her not choosing to accept be an open alternative at this point, before she chooses? Well, what conditions would have to hold, in order for Cathy *not* to choose to accept? For Cathy to avoid the choice to accept, at a minimum she would have *not* to choose to accept. In other words, a necessary condition for Cathy not choosing to accept is that very condition itself: *that Cathy will not choose to accept the offer*. As the Second Assumption says, that condition is a non-negotiable necessary condition for itself. Again, it is part of our example that Cathy *will* choose to accept. So a necessary condition of this *not* happening is *absent*, now and forever. The First Assumption of the argument says that when any necessary condition for something not happening is absent, the thing is fixed and unalterable. So it follows from the two assumptions that Cathy's actual choice is already fixed and unalterable before she makes it.

The same reasoning applies equally well to any apparently open possibility, whether or not choice is involved. Concerning any actual thing at any time, some necessary condition for not having that thing is absent—if nothing else, the missing necessary condition is the very condition of not having the thing at the time. So the argument arrives at the following conclusion.

Fully Fatalistic Conclusion. All actual entities, events, and circumstances, past, present, and future, are fixed and unalterable down to the last detail.

To begin a critical examination of the Necessary Conditions argument, let's rethink the explanation presented earlier of why we regard past facts as fixed and unalterable. We observed that my finishing a mile run is not an open possibility at times like now when I haven't been running. We also observed that my having run almost a mile is a necessary condition for my finishing a mile, and that condition is absent. But is the *absence* of a necessary condition really the explanation of why I cannot now finish a mile run? Here is a rival explanation. To finish a mile run now, I'd have to cause different things to have happened prior to now. I'd have somehow to cause it to be the case that I have been running. But as a matter of fact, I *cannot* do anything now that would cause me to have been running, nor can anything else now cause me to have been running.[3] This *incapacity* to supply the needed condition is why I can't finish a mile run now.

Once this account is offered, it seems a better explanation. Generally, we regard the events of the past as not subject to any current causal influence. Our confidence in the fixity of the past derives from that.

Even if this is a better account of why we think that past facts are unalterable, so far this is no objection to the core of the Necessary Conditions argument. It is no reason to deny the claim of the First Assumption that something is unalterable when a necessary condition of an alteration is absent. But once we don't need that claim to understand the fixity of the

---

[3] Our chapter about time defends the *possibility* of backward causation. The topic there is whether there *could have been* a reality where causes run backwards in time. Even if such an alternative reality is possible, this does not tell us what causes are *actually available.*

past, we can see that the claim is doubtful on its own. Let's revisit Cathy's choice. We must concede that, whichever choice Cathy makes, some necessary condition of the alternative is *absent*. Does that absence, all by itself, make her stuck with her actual choice? It seems not. She need not be stuck with it, if the missing condition is *available* to her. If she is *able* to supply all missing necessary conditions, then no necessary condition stands in her way.

We have no reason to doubt that Cathy is able to supply the needed conditions. The necessary condition discussed, that of her not choosing to accept the offer, *seems* available as she considers the choice. Maybe there is some hidden reason why it is not really available. But the reason is *not* just that her non-acceptance is a necessary condition, and it is absent. Analogously, the mere absence of, say, a person, doesn't imply that the person is *unavailable*. The person may be ready and waiting to be present. Likewise, we have no good reason to think that the mere absence of a necessary condition for something locks in its unavailability. This undercuts the reasonableness of the First Assumption of the Necessary Conditions argument.

So the argument is in trouble. The mere absence of a necessary condition does not seem to *guarantee* its unavailability. The First Assumption might be defended on another basis. It could be contended that absent necessary conditions never *actually are available*. This would be enough. We would be just as stuck with the actual situation if the necessary conditions for something else were never in fact available. Are they ever available?

Consider this challenge: If there are available alternatives that make for open possibilities, then how come no allegedly open possibility has ever been *realized*? Never once has something true at a time turned into something that was untrue at that very time. No truth was ever actually avoided. So why think that the makings for such a thing are actually *available*?

In confronting these questions, we should think carefully about what we are denying if we deny that all is fixed and settled. If we say that an actual future truth is not fixed and settled, then we are *not* saying or implying that something true at a time can be made untrue *too*. We are saying, concerning something true in the future, that it has some potential to be untrue *instead*. We are thinking that some truths have an *unrealized* potential to be *just* untrue, *never* true. To defend this thought, we need not directly answer the questions just raised. We need not look for something that has the status of being true at a time and show how it could become *also* untrue or it could *change into* being untrue at the time. Yet the challenge posed by the questions asks us for an example of something true at a time that *realizes* the potential to be untrue at the time. So we need not meet this challenge.

How might we defend our belief in the existence of the potential, if not with the sort of examples that the challenge asks for? We could start by arguing that some future events— maybe choices, maybe physically undetermined events—are not necessitated in any known way. This would include arguing that the fatalists' efforts to prove otherwise fail. Also, we might find evidence that certain pairs of scenarios are duplicates of one another in every way that seems relevant. Yet in one member of the pair, one of our candidates for being an open possibility occurs; in the other member of the pair, the other alternative occurs. If we find such pairs, then in each case the paired duplicate argues that nothing made the one possibility occur rather than the other—it just chanced to happen one way. For instance, two flips of a coin, controlled in every known way to be exact duplicate flips in exact duplicate conditions, might be found to result in the coin landing on different sides. Wouldn't it be most reasonable to say that each flip had a chance to end up the other way? Finally, we might have a well-confirmed scientific theory that implies that some outcomes remain undetermined until they occur. These are reasons that we can have to think that there are open possibilities.

God Knows

Maybe an all-knowing God exists.[4] If so, does that make fatalism true too? Metaphysical fatalism might seem to follow readily from the existence of God, using the following argument.

> *First Assumption*: If God knows everything, then God knows in advance all truths about the whole future.

That seems safe, though we shall see that some have objected to it.

> *Second Assumption*: If God knows any given truth about the future, then any potential for that truth to be untrue would be a potential for God to be mistaken about it.

To see what the Second Assumption says, suppose that God knows that a particular flipped coin *will* land heads up. According to the Second Assumption, any potential for the coin *not* to land heads up would be a potential for God to have the mistaken belief that it will land heads up. The heads-up outcome is what God thinks and knows in advance. So if the future turned out the other way, the Second Assumption implies that God would still have this same belief and it would be untrue. We'll soon think more about that assumption.

> *Final Assumption*: It is impossible for God to be mistaken about anything.

---

[4] We investigate this in our 'God' chapter.

We can take it for granted that the Final Assumption is correct because that is the sort of God we are considering—a God who is never mistaken under any possible conditions.

>*Conditionally Fatalistic Conclusion*: If God knows everything, then the whole future is fixed and unalterable.

This conclusion does not assert any fatalism. Deriving fatalism about the future would require the added assumption that an all-knowing God does exist. Still, it is interesting enough to consider whether or not the existence of an all-knowing God *implies* that the whole future is fixed.

One line of opposition to the God Knows argument holds that, contrary to the First Assumption, God knows everything without knowing anything in advance. The opponent claims that God is outside of the time in which we exist—that is, the sequential time of before and after, the time of past, present, and future. God exists 'in eternity'. Eternity is not in sequential time. Eternity is not before, during, or after anything. So God does not know anything 'in advance', since this requires existing in time before something happens and knowing that it will happen. God exists in eternity instead. The objection concludes that this allows God to know everything without having any advance knowledge.

Existence outside of past, present, and future is difficult to understand. Whatever such existence amounts to, though, it does not seem to ruin the core of the God Knows argument. The argument essentially relies on God having *exhaustive* knowledge, not *advance* knowledge. To see this, we can replace 'in advance' in the argument with 'in eternity'. To the extent that we can understand the resulting reasoning, it seems to have the same merits as the original. Suppose that God knows in eternity what is in our future—the future relative to us now. If so, then any potential for our future to be otherwise is a potential for something God knows to be untrue. The God Knows argument tries to persuade us that potential of that sort implies an impossible mistake by God. If the argument succeeds, then we could not avoid the conclusion by locating God in eternity. So this is not a promising source of doubt about the reasoning.

What about the Second Assumption of the God Knows argument? It says that if there is some potential for a true predictive statement not to be true, even though God knows it to be true (in advance or in eternity), then that is a potential for God to make a mistake. This claim is doubtful. Why would God be stuck believing something, whether or not it was true? God's knowledge could be more flexible.

For instance, maybe God knows all by 'seeing' all. Thus, God knows how things will be in our future by perfectly perceiving how things are at later times. Perception of a fact always derives from that fact. So God's perceptual knowledge of future facts derives from the facts perceived. If God knows by perception how our future will be, then God derives from our future complete information about it.

If this is how God's knowledge of our future works, then a potential for things to *be* otherwise in our future would be accompanied by a potential for God to have *perceived* otherwise. The future facts would have been different and God would have perceived them to be facts. Had things been otherwise, God would have derived different future information (in advance or in eternity). God would have known the alternative truths instead of having any mistaken beliefs.

This casts doubt on the Second Assumption of the God Knows argument. It shows us that one sort of knowledge by God of the future, combined with the existence of some potential for an alternative future truth, does *not* imply the possibility of God making a mistake. The combination only implies a potential for something that is actually known by God to have been untrue—not a potential for it to have been mistakenly believed by God.

A Final Note

None of the arguments for metaphysical fatalism has turned out to seem successful. Nonetheless, a popular fatalistic saying remains appealing: 'What will be, will be.' There is no denying that this states a fact. Did we overlook the wisdom here in our search for support for fatalism?

Actually, there is no metaphysical fatalism in the saying. It does not say that anything *has to be*. People do sometimes use these words to express an attitude of resignation toward whatever the future holds. But any good basis for that attitude is something beyond the sheer content of the saying. The fact that it states does not warrant any attitude, fatalistic resignation or otherwise. It claims nothing one way or the other about whether we control the future or whether the future is already settled. It simply says: however things will be, that is how they will be—however they get to be that way. This is not fatalism.

People sometimes take the saying to assert that whatever is *destined* to be, will be. That is not what it literally says, since it does not mention destiny. But people do take it that way. It sounds more fatalistic on this interpretation. It really isn't, though. It does not say how much of the future is destined, *if any*. Everyone, including those who deny all destiny, can agree that 'whatever' is destined, will be. Those who deny all destiny can consistently add that this is an empty truth, because nothing is destined.

'What will be, will be' is a good thing to say, for all that. It often comforts people. It just doesn't give us any reason to accept metaphysical fatalism.

FURTHER READING

This chapter opposes arguments for metaphysical fatalism. The following are a couple of works by defenders of fatalistic arguments. They include arguments that we have discussed. Several editions of a book by Richard Taylor are listed, because his defense of fatalism changes notably in succeeding editions of his book.

Steven M. Cahn, *Fate, Logic and Time* (Ridgeview, 1967).

Richard Taylor, 'Fate', in *Metaphysics* (Prentice-Hall, 1963, 1974, 1983, 1992).

An issue with close connections to fatalism is the compatibility of God's knowledge of our future with our having freedom. Here is a collection of essays about that.

John Martin Fisher (ed.), *God, Foreknowledge, and Freedom* (Stanford, 1989).

*

CHAPTER 3

Time

Theodore Sider

The Flow of Time

It is strange to question the nature of time, given how fundamental time is to our experience. As a child I wondered whether
fish are conscious of water or whether they experience it uncon-
sciously, as we experience the air we breathe. Time is even more
ubiquitous than water or air: every thought and experience takes
place in time. Questioning the nature of time can be dizzying.

Yet it is worth questioning. The ordinary conception of time,
once you start to think about it, seems to make no sense! For we
ordinarily conceive of time as being something that *moves*. 'Time
flows like a river.' 'Time marches on.' 'Time flies.' 'As time goes
by.' 'The past is gone.' 'Time waits for no one.' 'Time stood still.'
These clichés capture how we tend to think about time. Time
moves, and we are caught up in its inexorable flow. The problem
with this way of thinking is that time is the standard by which
motion is defined; how then could time itself move? This is
metaphysics at its best. Look at the world hard enough, and
even the most mundane things are revealed as mysterious and
wonderful.

Let's examine this idea of time's motion, or flow, more carefully, by comparing it to the motion of ordinary objects. What does it mean to say that a *train* moves? Simply that the train is located at one place at one moment in time and at other places at later moments in time (see Figure 1). At time t_1, the train is in Boston. At later times t_2, t_3, and t_4, the train is located at places further south: New York, Philadelphia, and finally, Washington. The motion of the train is defined by reference to time: the train moves by being located at different places at different times. If at every moment the train stayed in the same place—Boston, say—then we would say that the train did not move.

Ordinary objects move with respect to time. So if time itself moves, it must move with respect to some other sort of time. But what would that other time be?

The way in which time seems to move is by the *present moment's* moving. Initially the present moment is noon. Later the present is 3.00 p.m. Still later it is 6.00 p.m., and then 9.00 p.m.,

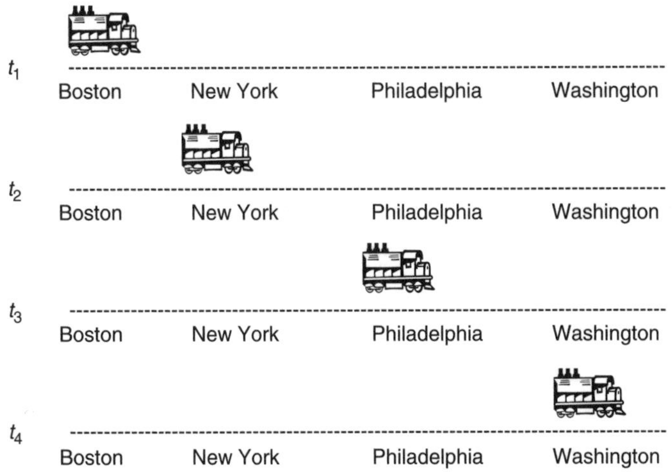

t_1	Boston	New York	Philadelphia	Washington
t_2	Boston	New York	Philadelphia	Washington
t_3	Boston	New York	Philadelphia	Washington
t_4	Boston	New York	Philadelphia	Washington

Fig. 1. The movement of a train defined by reference to time

and so on. Since motion is defined by reference to time, the present moment, if it is moving, must have these four different locations at four different times, t_1, t_2, t_3, and t_4 (Figure 2), just as the moving train had four different locations at four different times. But the diagram is confusing. It mentions the times noon, 3.00, 6.00, and 9.00, but it also mentions four other times, t_1, t_2, t_3, and t_4. These are the times with respect to which the present moment is moving. What are these other times? In what sort of time does time itself move?

One possibility is that t_1, t_2, t_3, and $t_{\pm 4}$ are part of a *different* sort of time, call it **hypertime**. Just as trains move with respect to something else (time), time itself moves with respect to something else (hypertime). Most motion takes place with respect to the familiar timeline, but time itself moves with respect to another timeline, hypertime.

Hypertime is a bad idea. You can't simply stop there; you need more, and More and MORE. Hypertime is supposed to be a sort of time. So if ordinary time moves, surely hypertime moves as well. So hypertime must move with respect to yet another sort of

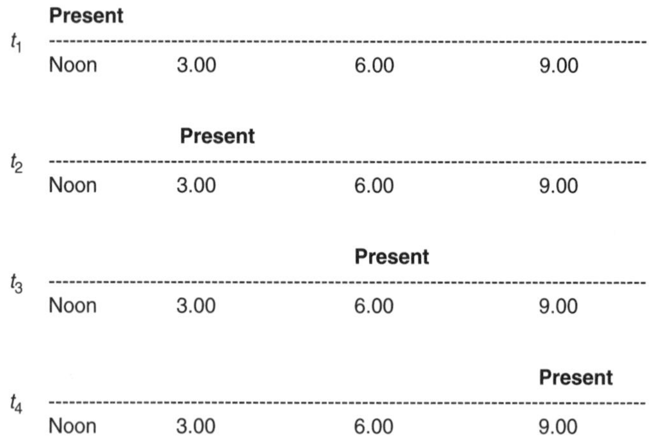

Fig. 2. The moving of the present moment

time, hyper-hyper time. That time must also move, which introduces hyper-hyper-hyper time. And so on. We are stuck with believing in an infinite series of different kinds of time. That's a little much. I can't *prove* that this infinite series does not exist, but surely there are better options. Let's see if we took a wrong turn somewhere.

Instead of being part of hypertime, perhaps t_1, t_2, t_3, and t_4 are just part of ordinary time. In particular, t_1, t_2, t_3, and t_4 could just be the times noon, 3.00, 6.00, and 9.00. According to this view, time moves with respect to itself. Is that plausible?

Although it's nice to be rid of hypertime, there is something strange about this picture. It's not that it isn't *true*. Noon is indeed present at noon, 3.00 is present at 3.00, and so on. But these facts seem *trivial*, and therefore insufficient to capture a genuine flow of time. This can be brought out by comparing time to space, and comparing *present* to *here*. Consider the spatial locations on the train track connecting Boston to Washington. Anyone in Boston can truthfully say 'Boston is *here*'. Likewise, anyone in New York can say 'New York is here'. The same goes for Philadelphia and Washington. So Boston is 'here in Boston', New York is 'here in New York', and so on, just as noon is present at noon, 3.00 is present at 3.00, and so on. But space doesn't move. The line in space connecting Boston with Washington is static. The mere fact that members of a series are located at themselves does not make that series move, whether that series consists of points of time or locations in space.

The Space-Time Theory

Time's motion has us all tangled up in knots. Maybe the problem is with that idea itself. According to some philosophers and scientists, our ordinary conception of time as a flowing river is hopelessly confused, and must be replaced with the **space-time theory**, according to which *time is like space*.

Graphs of motion from high-school physics represent time as just another dimension alongside the spatial dimensions. The graph pictured here (Figure 3) represents a particle that moves through time in one spatial dimension. This particle begins at place 2 in space at the initial time 1, then moves toward place 3, slows down and stops at time 2, and finally moves back to place 2 at time 3. Each point in this two-dimensional graph represents a time *t* (the horizontal coordinate of the point) and a location in space *p* (the vertical coordinate). The curve drawn represents the particle's motion. When the curve passes through a point (*t*, *p*), that means that the particle is located at place *p* at time *t*.

A more complicated graph (Figure 4) represents time alongside two spatial dimensions. (It would be nice to represent all three spatial dimensions, but that would require a four-dimensional graph and so a much more expensive book.) These more complicated graphs are called **space-time diagrams**. (Even the high-school physics graph is a simpler kind of diagram of space-time.) Space-time diagrams can be used to represent all of history; everything that has ever happened or ever will happen can be fit into a space-time diagram somewhere. This particular

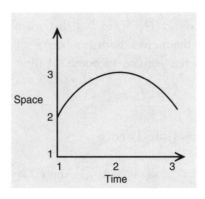

Fig. 3. High-school physics graph of a particle moving through time

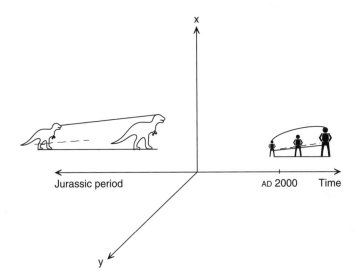

Fig. 4. Space-time diagram

diagram represents a dinosaur in the distant past and a person who is born in AD 2000. These objects stretch out horizontally in the graph because they last over time in reality, and time is the horizontal axis on the graph: the objects exist at different points along the horizontal time axis. They stretch out in the other two dimensions on the graph because dinosaurs and people take up space in reality: the objects exist at different points along the vertical, spatial, axes.

In addition to the dinosaur and the person themselves, some of their **temporal parts** are also represented in the diagram. A temporal part of an object at a time is a temporal cross-section of that object; it is that-object-at-that-time. Consider the temporal part of the person in 2000. ♀ This object is the exact same *spatial size* as the person in 2000. But the temporal part is not the same *temporal size* as the person; the temporal part exists only in 2000 whereas the person exists at later times as well. The person herself is the sum total of all her temporal parts:

Notice how the person is tapered: the earlier temporal parts (those on the left of the diagram) are smaller than the later ones. This represents the person's growth over time.[1]

In contrast to the ordinary conception of moving or flowing time, then, the space-time theory says that reality consists of a single unified space-time, which contains all of the past, present, and future. Time is just one of the dimensions of space-time, alongside the three spatial dimensions, just as it appears to be in the space-time diagrams. Time does not flow; time is like space.

Well, time isn't *completely* like space. For one thing, there are three spatial dimensions but only one temporal dimension. And time has a special *direction*: past to future. Space has no such direction. We do have words for certain spatial directions: up, down, north, south, east, west, left, right. But these are not directions built into space itself. Rather, these words pick out different directions depending on who says them. 'Up' means away from the earth's center on a line that passes through the speaker; 'North' means toward the Arctic pole from the speaker; 'Left' picks out different directions depending on which way the speaker is facing. In contrast, the past to future direction is the same for everyone, regardless of his or her location or orientation; it seems to be an intrinsic feature of time itself.

Still, according to the space-time theory, time and space are analogous in many ways. Here are three.

First, in terms of *reality*. Objects far away in space (other planets, stars, and so on) are obviously just as real as things here on Earth. We may not *know* as much about the far-away objects as we know about the things around here, but that doesn't make the far-away objects any less real. Likewise, objects far away in time are just as real as objects that exist now. Both past objects (e.g. dinosaurs) and future objects (human outposts on Mars, perhaps) exist, in addition to objects in the present.

[1] Temporal parts are discussed further at the end of Chapter 7.

Distant objects, whether temporally or spatially distant, all exist somewhere in space-time.

Second, in terms of *parts*. Material objects take up space by having different parts. My body occupies a certain region of space. Part of this region is occupied by my head, another by my torso; other parts of the region are occupied by my arms and legs. These parts may be called my spatial parts, since they are spatially smaller than I am. The corresponding fact about time is that an object lasts over a stretch of time by having different parts located at the different times within that stretch. These parts are the temporal parts mentioned above. These temporal parts are just as real objects as my spatial parts: my head, arms, and legs.

Third, in terms of *here* and *now*. If I say on the phone 'here it is raining' to a friend in California, and she replies 'here it is sunny' (Figure 5), which one of us is right? Where is the *real here*, California or New Jersey? The question is obviously misguided. There is no 'real here'. The word 'here' just refers to whatever place the person saying it happens to be. When *I* say 'here', it means New Jersey; when my friend says 'here', it means California. Neither place is *here* in any objective sense. California is here for my friend, New Jersey is here for me. The space-time theory

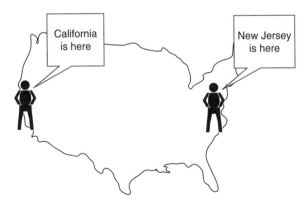

Fig. 5. Where is the 'real here'?

says an analogous thing about time: just as there is no objective here, so there is no objective *now*. If I say 'It is now 2005', and in 1606 Guy Fawkes said 'It is now 1606', each statement is correct (Figure 6). There is no single, real, objective 'now'. The word 'now' just refers to the time at which the speaker happens to be located.

Arguments Against the Space-Time Theory: Change, Motion, Causes

We have met two theories of time. Which is true? Does time flow? Or is time like space?

The space-time theory avoids the paradoxes of time's flow; that counts in its favor. But the believer in time's flow will retort that the space-time theory throws the baby out with the bath-

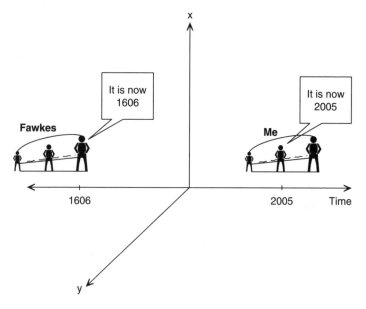

Fig. 6. 'Now' for me and for Guy Fawkes

water: it makes time *too much* like space. For starters, she may say that the alleged analogies between space and time suggested in the last section don't really hold:

> Past and future objects do *not* exist: the past is gone, and the future is yet to be. Things do *not* have temporal parts: at any time, the *whole* object is present, not just a temporal part of it; there are no past or future bits left out. And 'now' is *not* like 'here': the present moment is special, unlike the bit of space around here.

Each of these claims could take up a whole chapter of its own. But time is short, so let's consider three other ways the defender of time's flow might argue that time is not like space. First, regarding *change*:

> Compare change with what we might call 'spatial hetero-geneity'. Change is having different properties at different times. A person who changes height starts out short and then becomes taller. Spatial heterogeneity, in contrast, is having different properties at different *places*. A highway is bumpy at some places, smooth at others; narrow at some places, wide at others. Now, if time is just like space, then having different properties at different times (change) is no different from having different properties at different places (spatial heterogeneity). Look back at the space-time dia-gram. Change is variation from left to right on the diagram, along the temporal axis. Spatial heterogeneity is variation along either of the two spatial dimensions. The two are analogous, according to the space-time theory. But that's not right! Spatial heterogeneity is wholly different from change. The spatially heterogeneous highway doesn't *change*. It just sits there.

Second, regarding *motion*:

Things can move any which way in space; there's no particular direction in which they are constrained to travel. But the same is not true for time. Moving back and forth in time makes no sense. Things can only travel forward in time.

Third, regarding *causes*:

Events at any place can cause events at any other place; we can affect what goes on in any region of space. But events can't cause events at just any other time: later events never cause earlier events. Although we can affect the future, we cannot affect the past. The past is fixed.

The first objection is right that the space-time theory makes change somewhat similar to spatial heterogeneity. But so what? They're not *exactly* the same: one is variation over time, the other is variation over space. And the claim that change and spatial heterogeneity are *somewhat* similar is perfectly reasonable. So the first objection may be flatly rejected.

The second objection is more complicated. 'Things move back and forth in space, but not back and forth in time'—is this really a disanalogy between time and space? Suppose we want to know, for a certain true statement about space, whether the analogous statement is true of time. The twentieth-century American philosopher Richard Taylor argued that we must be careful to construct a statement about time that really is analogous to the statement about space. In particular, we must *uniformly reverse ALL references to time and space* to get the analogous statement. And when we do, Taylor argued, we will see that time and space are more analogous than they initially seemed.

To illustrate. Our true statement about space is this:

Some object moves back and forth in space.

Before we can reverse the references to time and space in this statement, we need to locate all those references, including any that are not completely explicit. For instance, the word 'moves' conceals a reference to time. When these references are made explicit, our statement becomes:

Moving back and forth in space: Some object is at spatial point p_1 at time t_1, point p_2 at time t_2, and point p_1 at time t_3.

(See Figure 7.) Now we're in a position to construct the analogous statement about time—to reverse *all* references to time and space. To do so, we simply change each reference to a time into a reference to a point in space, and each reference to a point in space into a reference to a time. This is what we get:

Moving back and forth in time: Some object is at time t_1 at spatial point p_1, time t_2 at point p_2, and at time t_1 at point p_3.

And we get the graph for this new statement (Figure 8) by swapping the 'Time' and 'Space' labels on the Figure 7.

Our question now is: is this second statement correct? Can an object 'move back and forth in time' in this sense? The answer is in fact *yes*, for a fairly humdrum reason. To make this easy to see, let's make the 'moving back and forth in time' graph look like our earlier diagrams by flipping it so that its temporal axis is horizontal (see Figure 9). It should be clear that the diagram represents an object that is first, at t_1, located at *two* places, p_1 and

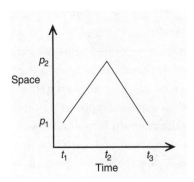

Fig. 7. Moving back and forth in space

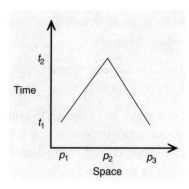

Fig. 8. Moving back and forth in time, temporal axis vertical

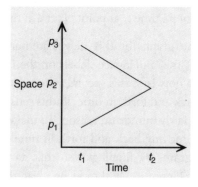

Fig. 9. Moving back and forth in time, temporal axis horizontal

p_3, and then, at t_2, is located at just one place, p_2. This sounds stranger than it really is. Think of a clapping pair of hands. At first the two hands are separated—one is located at place p_1, the other at p_3. Then the hands move toward each other and make contact. The pair of hands is now located at place p_2. Finally, suppose the pair of hands disappears at time t_2. This kind of scenario is what the diagram is representing.

So things *can* 'move back and forth in time', if that statement is understood as being truly analogous to 'moving back and forth in space'. We were deceived into thinking otherwise by neglecting to reverse *all* references to time and space. The statement 'things move back and forth in space' contains an implicit *reference dimension*, namely time, for it is with respect to time that things move in space. When we construct the statement 'things move back and forth in time', we must change the reference dimension from time to space. When we do, the resulting statement is something that can indeed be true.

The third objection is the most challenging and interesting. It is true that we do not actually observe 'backwards causation', that is, the causation of earlier events by later events. This represents a *de facto* asymmetry between space and time—an asymmetry in the world as it actually is. But a deeper question is whether this asymmetry is built into the nature of time itself, or whether it is just a function of the way the world happens to be. The question is: *could* there be backwards causation? *Could* our actions now causally affect the past?

If time is truly like space, then the answer must be *yes*. Just as events can cause events anywhere else in space, so too events can in principle cause other events anywhere in time, even at earlier times. But this has a very striking consequence. If backwards causation is possible, then *time travel*, as depicted in books and movies, ought to be possible as well, for it ought to be possible to cause ourselves to be present in the past.

Time travel may never *in fact* occur. Perhaps time travel will never be technologically feasible, or perhaps the laws of physics prevent time travel. Philosophy cannot settle questions about physics or technology; for speculation on such matters, a better guide is your friendly neighborhood physicist or engineer. But if time is like space, there should be no prohibition *coming from the concept of time itself*: time travel should at least be conceptually possible. But is it?

A familiar kind of time travel story begins as follows: 'In 1985, Marty McFly enters a time machine, sets the controls for 1955, pushes the button, waits, and then arrives in 1955 . . . ' Any time travel story must contain this much: the use of some sort of time travel device and subsequent arrival in the past. But even this much seems to conceal a contradiction. The troublesome bit is the end: 'and *then* arrives in 1955'. The suggestion is that McFly *first* pushes the button, and *second* arrives in 1955. But he pushes the button in 1985, which is *after* 1955.

This is an example of a so-called paradox of time travel. One attempts to tell a coherent story involving time travel, but ends up contradicting oneself. Saying that McFly arrives in 1955 both after and before he pushes the button is contradicting oneself. And if there is no way to tell a time travel story without self-contradiction, then time travel is conceptually impossible.

This first paradox can be avoided. Is the arrival after or before the pushing of the button? *Before*—1955 is before 1985. What about 'and *then*'? Well, all that means is that McFly *experiences* the arrival as being after the button-pressing. Normal people (i.e. non-time travelers) experience events as occurring in the order in which they truly occur, whereas time travelers experience things out of order. In the sequence of McFly's experiences, 1985 comes before 1955. That's a very strange thing, to be sure, but it does not seem conceptually incoherent. (What determines the order of McFly's experiences? Later members of the sequence of his experiences contain memories of, and are caused by, earlier members of the sequence. When McFly experiences 1955, he has memories of 1985, and his 1985 experiences directly causally affect his 1955 experiences.)

Yet a more potent paradox lurks. Let's continue the story from *Back to the Future*: 'Back in 1955, the dashing McFly inadvertently attracts his mother, overshadowing his nerdy father. As the union of his parents becomes less and less likely, McFly begins to fade away into nothingness.' The problem is that a time traveler could undermine his own existence. He could cause his parents never to meet; he could even kill them before he is ever born. But then where did he come from? Back to paradox!

That McFly begins to fade away into nothingness shows that the writers of *Back to the Future* were aware of the problem. But the fade-out solves nothing. Suppose McFly fades out completely after preventing his parents from meeting. He still existed before fading out (it was he, after all, who prevented his parents from meeting). Where then did he come from in the first place? Whatever its literary merits, as a work of philosophy *Back to the Future* fails miserably.

Let's not be too hard on careless screen-writers and authors. (We can't all be philosophers.) Though it's not easy, paradox-free time travel stories can be told. The movie *Terminator* is an excellent example (spoilers included):[2]

> In the future, machines take over the world and nearly destroy the human race. But the machines are eventually thwarted by the human leader John Connor. On the verge of defeat, the machines fight back by sending a machine, a 'Terminator', back to the past to kill John Connor's mother, Sarah Connor, before John is born. John Connor counters by sending one of his men, Kyle Reese, back to the past to protect Sarah Connor. The Terminator nearly succeeds, but in the end Reese stops him. (Reese dies, but not before impregnating Connor's mother, Sarah Connor. The baby, we later learn, grows up to be John Connor himself!)

This story never contradicts itself. It would if the Terminator killed Sarah Connor, since we are told in the beginning of the story that Sarah Connor lived and had a son, John Connor,

---

[2] *Terminator 1*, that is. *Terminator 2* appears to be incoherent. It says in the beginning that Cyberdyne systems learned the technology behind Skynet by studying the hand of the corpse of a T-800 Terminator from the future. Then at the end, after the T-800 is melted (Schwarzenegger's thumbs-up to Furlong), the movie suggests that Skynet is never created and Judgment Day is avoided. Where then did the time-traveling Terminators come from? *Terminator 3* does better: it never suggests that Judgment Day is avoided. Yet there are remaining questions, for instance about the true date of Judgment Day. *Terminator 1* is by far the best of the three, from a philosophical (as well as cinematic) point of view.

whose future exploits are the cause of the presence of the Terminator in the past. But since Sarah Connor survives, the story remains consistent.

The failure of *some* time travel stories (such as *Back to the Future*) to remain consistent shows nothing, since other consistent stories can be told. The similarity of time and space has survived: there is no conceptual impossibility with backwards causation and time travel.

There are numerous close calls in *Terminator*. Again and again, Sarah Connor narrowly escapes death. It would appear that on any of these occasions, she could easily have died. Yet we know that she must survive, because her son is John Connor. So it seems that she is not really in danger; she cannot die. But there is the Terminator in front of her. The danger seems very real. Back into paradox?

Not at all. What is strange about a time travel story is that we are told the end of the story first. We, the audience, learn early on that John Connor exists in the future. Later we find his mother endangered before he is ever born. We, the audience, know she will survive (if we trust the screen-writers to be consistent!), but that does not mean that *in the story* her danger is unreal.

A very peculiar thing arises when the time traveler himself knows how the story will end. Think of Reese. He knows that the Terminator will fail, since he knows that John Connor exists: it was Connor that sent him back to the past. Yet he fears for Sarah Connor's life, works hard to protect her, and in the end gives his life to save her. Why doesn't he just walk away and save himself? He *knows* that Sarah Connor is going to survive.

Or does he? He *thinks* he remembers serving a man called John Connor. He *thinks* he remembers Connor defeating the machines. He *thinks* Connor's mother was named Sarah. He *thinks* this woman he's defending is the same Sarah Connor. He *thinks* this woman has not yet had children. So he's got lots of evidence that this woman he's defending will survive. But then he sees the

Terminator advance. He sees it effortlessly killing everyone in its path, searching for someone named Sarah Connor. Now it advances on the woman he's defending. It raises its gun. Reese's confidence that this woman will survive now wavers. Perhaps she is not John Connor's mother after all. Or, if he's sure of that, perhaps she's already had a child. Or, if he's quite sure of that, perhaps he's made some other mistake. Perhaps all of his apparent memories from the future are delusions! Such self-doubt is ordinarily far-fetched, but it becomes increasingly reasonable with each step of the Terminator. As certain as he once was that Sarah Connor will survive, he has become equally certain about the danger presented by the Terminator: 'It can't be bargained with! It can't be reasoned with! It doesn't feel pity, or remorse, or fear. And it absolutely will not stop, ever, until you are dead!' He thinks 'I'd better be sure.' He raises his gun.

FURTHER READING

Peter van Inwagen and Dean Zimmerman (eds.), *Metaphysics: The Big Questions* (Blackwell, 1998): this anthology contains a number of readings on time (as well as readings on many other metaphysical topics.) Some highlights: 'Time', by J. M. E. McTaggart, makes the shocking claim that time is unreal! Two articles by A. N. Prior argue against the space-time theory. 'The Space-Time World', by J. J. C. Smart, defends the space-time theory. 'The Paradoxes of Time Travel', by David Lewis, argues that time travel is possible.

This article by Richard Taylor lays out a fascinating series of analogies between space and time: 'Spatial and Temporal Analogies and the Concept of Identity', *Journal of Philosophy*, 52 (1955), 599–612.

In addition to the conceptual issues about time travel discussed in this chapter, there are many interesting scientific issues as well. The following article is available online: Frank Arntzenius and Tim Maudlin, 'Time Travel and Modern Physics', http://plato.stanford.edu/entries/time-travel-phys/

CHAPTER 4

God

Earl Conee

'Religion is entirely a matter of opinion, of course, and you are as entitled to your religious opinions as I am to mine.' We've all heard that. We may have said it ourselves. It seems to be a safe and sensible judgment, until we stop trying to be so agreeable and take it seriously. Then it starts to look like a premature judgment, maybe even a dogmatic one.

When a disputed topic is entirely a matter of opinion, there is no better reason to take one side than another. So if religion is entirely a matter of opinion, then either the reasons for and against any religious view balance out evenly, or there are no reasons at all. Before we go along with the thought that religion is like that, shouldn't we look to see what the reasons are?

Religion and metaphysics overlap on the question of God's existence. It is a metaphysical matter because part of metaphysics, **ontology**, concerns the most basic kinds of beings. God is basic. For one thing, God is the creator of the universe, if God exists. It would be of tremendous metaphysical interest to learn that a great portion of reality depends for its existence on the creative choice of one being.

Several lines of reasoning are aimed at establishing that God exists. We'll investigate three sorts of arguments where many of the surrounding issues are metaphysical.

Getting It All Started

Effects

Our first version of an argument for God's existence relies on one fact about the world. The fact is that some things are caused to happen. Many things that are taking place now are clearly effects of various causes. This includes things that are happening to you right now. You see these words as an effect of light that is beamed to your eyes and you understand these words as an effect of your learning English and applying your knowledge of it.

Okay, so there are effects. What is the connection to God's existence?

We next observe that the causes of effects are themselves caused. Those causes in turn have their causes, and so on.

The reasoning from this point that gets us to God's existence is not supposed to rely on anything that we find out by observing the world around us. We are supposed to see its force by thinking about the relation of cause and effect. First we note that the sequences of cause and effect might go back indefinitely. But could this go on without limit? The argument asserts that each causal sequence must have gotten started. There must have been a first cause that was not caused, to get each sequence into existence. Thomas Aquinas was the major medieval proponent of this sort of argument. Aquinas observed that, if you take away the cause, then you take away the effects. We see effects. He inferred that there must be some first cause of the existing effects. The argument concludes that the first cause of all is the creator of the universe, God.

The argument proceeds in two phases. The **premises** of the argument are the assumptions that it relies on. The **conclusion** of each phase is the claim that is supposed to be proven by that phase.

First Cause Argument

Phase 1

> *Premise1*: There are effects.
> *Premise2*: Any effect derives eventually from a first cause.
> *Conclusion1*: There is a first cause.

The second phase builds on the first. It starts with the conclusion that Phase 1 is supposed to prove. It adds another assumption and draws the First Cause argument's final conclusion.

Phase 2

> *Conclusion1*: There is a first cause.
> *Premise3*: If there is a first cause, then it is God.
> *Conclusion2*: God exists.

We have to select ways to understand 'God' and 'exists'. People mean various things by 'God.' Sometimes someone's 'God' is whoever the person idolizes. It might be the person's favorite musician. This meaning is no good for present purposes. It is not a major metaphysical matter whether or not any given musician exists (however major a musical matter it is). In contrast, it is metaphysically huge to find out about the existence of a being like this: a creator of the universe who is all-knowing, all-powerful, and morally perfect. We'll understand 'God' so that **God is** a being who is all-knowing, all-powerful, morally perfect, and the creator, if 'God' applies at all. By using the word only for a being with these extreme attributes, we make the issue of God's existence a topic of metaphysical significance and we use a meaning that is recognizable to those in Western religious traditions.

We'll understand 'exists' in a broad way. 'Exists' applies to anything that is in reality at all, whether past, present, or future, whether in space or not. What 'exists' does not apply to are merely apparent realities, the merely mythical, the illusory, the fictional.

An argument relies on its premises. They must be entirely reasonable to believe if the argument is to establish its conclusion. If there is some serious unresolved doubt about a premise, then the argument does not prove its conclusion.

Let's consider Premise2 ('P2' for short). The claim made by P2—that any sequence of cause and effect must have gotten started—holds a powerful grip on many people. It can seem just obvious that a series of things must have a first one. This grip loosens, though, when we try to spell out anything that would justify this claim. Exactly why can't each cause in a series have its own cause, with no beginning?

'No beginning' must be rightly understood. It just means that nothing is first in the series. There are familiar precedents for this. The series of numbers known as the integers has no first one. The integers include -1, which is preceded by -2, which is preceded by -3, and so on. The integers go back infinitely.

This infinity is not mind-boggling. We don't have to think of all of the integers separately. We understand the **infinity** adequately if we get the idea that each integer has a new integer as its predecessor. This arrangement is an understandable way for a sequence to exist while having 'no beginning'.

We see how the negative integers are arranged. Why couldn't causes and effects be arranged that way too? Why couldn't there be causes preceding effects backward in time infinitely into the past with no beginning? We cannot *picture* a whole infinite series like that. But we cannot do this picturing just because we have no way to picture the series' 'far end', since it has none. We still do understand the structure of the series, without a picture. So again, what reason do we have to deny the possibility of an infinite series of causes and effects that is structured in the same way? Nothing comes to mind.

This possibility undercuts the credibility of P2. P2 is supposed to be worth assuming because we are supposed to see the need for a first cause in order to have a causal sequence at all. P2 is doubtful if we don't see the need. And now we don't.

Trouble for the First Cause argument does not stop there. Phase 2 has a weakness as well, namely, P3. Suppose that a causal series has some first cause. P3 asserts that the first cause is God in particular. Why so?

Here is an answer: only almighty God is great enough for self-creation. So God can exist without having something else as a cause. Anything other than God has to have help in order to exist.

This answer assumes that each thing has to have a cause. It assumes that either the cause is something other than the effect, or the cause and the effect are one and the same. The answer claims that only God is fit to be a self-cause.

Why must each thing have any cause at all, though? It seems possible that something just happens to happen, without being caused at all. This possibility does not imply that anything is so powerful, or otherwise magnificent, that it causes itself. For all we can tell by thinking about causes and effects, it is possible that something just does happen in nature, without a cause, and it starts a causal series. Whether or not this ever actually happens, we don't seem to have any way to exclude it as impossible. So thinking about causes and effects does not give us any good basis to accept the claim made by P3 that any first cause is God.

There is a different defense of the claim that God is a special sort of cause. The new idea is that God is so great that God does not need to get caused into existence. In contrast, all lesser beings require help in order to exist.

But what does greatness have to do with getting caused? Why couldn't some tiny insignificant particle just pop into existence without anything making it exist, and then cause other things? The continuing appearance that this sort of first cause is possible casts doubt on P3

Maybe the need for God stems from a need for *explanations*. We could not correctly *explain why* a first cause just pops up, because there would be no explanation. Is that an objection to the possibility? Yes, if we have some assurance that everything has some correct explanation. The claim that there is an explanation for everything is known as the **Principle of Sufficient Reason**.

The Principle of Sufficient Reason requires an explanation for the existence of any first cause. The principle also raises questions about infinite causal series that do not have a first cause. Maybe each item *in* an infinite series is explained as an effect of prior causes. But according to the Principle of Sufficient Reason, that is not all that needs explaining. The *whole series* is something too. The principle requires an answer to the question of what explains why the whole series exists. Thus, first causes and infinite series of causes both require explanation, according to the principle.

A first response to the question that the principle raises about infinite causal series is that the whole series may have a *derivative* explanation. Perhaps when each event in the series has been explained, the combination of all of those explanations explains the whole thing.

That first response may seem fishy. Maybe each element in the series *causes* the next one. But do those causal facts entirely *explain* why that particular contingent series exists at all?

Suppose not. The Principle of Sufficient Reason requires that there be some explanation. But what assures us that this principle is true? When we think about how things might possibly have gone, it seems possible that some things just do exist with no explanation. Why not? The situation would be intellectually disappointing. But what guarantee do we have that intellectual satisfaction is always available? The Principle of Sufficient Reason declares that explanations always exist. Again, why believe it? The lofty title, 'Principle of Sufficient Reason', doesn't make the principle true. Anyway, it is easily matched. The **Principle of Insufficient Reason** says that some things have no explanation. The two principles conflict. Thinking about possibilities seems to tell us that each of the principles might have been true. Thinking about how things might be gives us no reason to believe the Principle of Sufficient Reason in particular.

If nothing assures us that the Principle of Sufficient Reason is true, then the principle does not help the argument. It does not justify our denying apparent possibilities that go against P3. For instance, it seems possible that everything started with the Big Bang, rather than God, and the Big Bang has no explanation. Until we have a sound basis for denying that any such possibility obtains, P3 is in doubt.

Dependents

Here is an interestingly different version of the argument. The new version is about a non-causal sort of dependence. **Ontological dependence** consists in one thing needing another simultaneously, in order to support its existence. The idea eludes precise definition, but it has one clear sort of illustration. Consider a tuna salad sandwich. At any given time, the sandwich derives its existence from the existence of the bread, the tuna salad, and any other ingredients that compose it. Without them, it would be nothing. The sandwich's ingredients do not *cause* it to exist. Rather, they give it existence directly. The sandwich 'ontologically depends' on its ingredients. Anything that does not depend in this way on any other entity is **ontologically independent**.

Using this idea of ontological dependence, the new version of the argument otherwise goes just like the previous one.

Ontological Dependence Argument

Phase 1

> *Premise1*: There are ontologically dependent things.
>
> *Premise2*: Anything ontologically dependent derives its existence eventually from something ontologically independent.
>
> *Conclusion1*: Something ontologically independent exists.

Phase 2

> *Conclusion1*: Something ontologically independent exists.
>
> *Premise3*: If something ontologically independent exists, then God exists.
>
> *Conclusion2*: God exists.

The claim made by P1 about the existence of ontological dependence is fully credible. Many things, such as a tuna sandwich, illustrate its truth. P2 is supposed to be true because an endless sequence of ontological dependence is supposed to be blatantly impossible. P3 is supposed to be true because only God is powerful and knowledgeable enough to be able to exist independently of all other entities.

We can be efficient here. The doubts about the Ontological Dependence argument parallel the doubts about the First Cause argument.

First, concerning P2, exactly why couldn't there be an endless sequence of ontological dependents? For instance, why not an endless sequence of bigger parts depending for their existence on ever smaller parts? The sheer infinity of the sequence does not make it inconceivable. We saw that much by considering the negative integers. If it is otherwise impossible, why is that? Until we see a good reason, P2 stands in doubt.

And why does only God qualify as ontologically independent? Suppose that there are point-sized physical particles that have no parts. Why think that they would have to depend on anything?

Until we have a good answer to this question, we have grounds to doubt that God is uniquely qualified for ontologically independence, as P3 claims.

Designing the World

When we stand back from the previous arguments and consider what they try to do, they seem amazingly ambitious. The only facts about the world around us that the arguments use are the facts that there are effects and that there are ontologically dependent things. Simple, abstract, neutral facts like those seem far removed from the existence of an all-knowing, all-powerful, morally perfect creator. It is no wonder that arguments on that meager basis turn out to fall short of proving God's existence.

The actual facts of the world are much more wonderful than just any old effects and dependencies that might have existed. Maybe some awe-inspiring facts about how things actually are can serve to establish God's existence.

Suppose that the whole universe was unplanned and purely accidental. What would it be like? We can apply to this question what we've observed about accidents. Accidents make messes. Car crashes, bridge collapses, and accidents generally, result in disarray. Yes, once in a while there is a fortunate accident where some structure happens to develop. Some inadvertently spilled paint occasionally forms some neat shape. But that is highly exceptional. And if the accidents keep coming, any structure in the situation eventually dissolves. Further accidental paint spills obliterate a pretty pattern. So, if the universe was entirely accidental, then our observations lead us to expect that it would display disorderly disarray, with the occasional pattern emerging briefly.

That is not what we find. Instead, we find an abundance of examples of organized structures resembling complex machines. The most impressive machine-like structures that we know of involve life. The examples range from the intricate interrelationships of components within single cells to the tremendous complexities of whole organisms and eco-systems. Matter at subcellular levels is also highly organized, from the structures of molecules to the structures of atoms and sub-atomic particles. On larger scales we find planetary systems, galaxies, and groups of galaxies.

We have experience with how order gets introduced. What we observe is that machine-like order is imposed by minds. We see such order arise by design in everything from simple tools to amazingly intricate systems like computers and ocean liners. We do observe mindless robotic devices at work on assembly lines, arranging materials into planes, trains, and automobiles. But highly intelligent planning always lies behind the whole setup.

What does this comparison tell us about the origin of the universe? Proponents of a design argument for God's existence contend that it makes a strong case for a divine mind behind the whole thing. They contend that the universe has machine-like structure throughout. They add that the only mind up to the task of planning all this is the mind of the divine creator, God.

First Version

Here is our first version of this reasoning, in two phases.

Demonstration by Design

Phase 1

Premise1: The universe exhibits intricate machine-like structure on every scale of space and time.
Premise2: The only possible way for the universe to exhibit such structure is for it to have been intelligently designed.

Conclusion1: The universe was intelligently designed.
Phase2

Conclusion1: The universe was intelligently designed.
Premise3: If the universe was intelligently designed, then it was designed by God.
Conclusion2: God exists.

P2 links the claim made by P1 about order in the universe to the conclusion of Phase 1 so that the conclusion follows inescapably. By doing this, though, P2 runs afoul of the possibility of the improbable. Consider the most orderly arrangement imaginable of the largest universe imaginable. Call it a **MOHU**, for 'Maximally Orderly Huge Universe'. If we somehow knew that we were in a MOHU, it would be ridiculous to assume that our MOHU happened to exist for no reason. That is so unlikely as to be virtually impossible. The problem for Phase 1 is that the accidental existence of a MOHU is only virtually impossible, not quite just plain impossible. No matter how much structure the MOHU has, its materials might possibly have happened to arrange themselves that way in a fluke random occurrence.

If we doubt this, our doubts can be worn away. We must acknowledge that some minimal structure could arise by chance, say, a simple shape arising from random fluctuations. How about just a little more structure? No doubt that is less likely, but still, it is a possibility. How about a little more, and more, and more? We find ourselves acknowledging the possibility of a structure exactly like a Rolls Royce arising at random. And we can't stop there. Only the likelihood decreases; we never reach any impossibility. Finally we have to admit that random typing by monkeys might possibly type out *Hamlet*. No defensible stopping place exists and we end up acknowledging the possibility of a chance MOHU. P2 denies this possibility, and that is bad for P2.

Second Version

There is an alternative version of the reasoning. Some arguments render their conclusions highly reasonable, though they offer something short of proof. If considerations of design could do that for the conclusion that God exists, it would be an important result. If we could be shown that affirming God's existence is as reasonable as denying that a MOHU happened by chance, then the claim that God exists would be very strongly supported. Even somewhat weaker support would be plenty interesting.

Let's return to what our observations show us about the origin of organized structure. Our observations make it grossly implausible that much machine-like order arose by accident. The claim that this order exists by accident seems a very poor *explanation* of it. In contrast, the claim that the order implements a planned design renders its existence understandable to us. Proponents of a design argument can offer God's design as the best explanation of the structure that we find in the universe. To capture this idea, we can replace P2 of the Demonstration from Design with a claim about explanation.

Best Explanation by Design

Phase 1

> *Premise1*: The universe exhibits machine-like structure on every scale of space and time.
> *Premise2e*: The best explanation of the universe exhibiting such structure is that the universe was intelligently designed.

So probably:

> *Conclusion1*: The universe was intelligently designed.

Phase 1 assumes that the best explanation of something is probably true. Phase 1 offers no proof that its conclusion C1 is true. But if it succeeds, then it makes for rational belief in C1.

Phase 2

> *Conclusion₁*: The universe was intelligently designed.
>
> *Premise₃*: If the universe was intelligently designed, then it was designed by God.
>
> *Conclusion₂*: God exists.

Not questioning P₁ for now, how credible is P₂e? Initially, it seems quite plausible. What could explain the high levels of order that we observe as well as the explanation claiming that the order resulted from an intelligent plan?

Here is a rival hypothesis: unplanned physical laws exist—laws of physics, chemistry, biology, and the other sciences—and these laws, operating on the physical materials in the universe, produce the high level of order. This natural sort of explanation does work. It gives an explanation of the machine-like organization that we observe in things like molecules, marsupials, and marshes. We can understand how some laws, operating on some materials that were in a position to develop into orderly arrangements by conforming to the laws, would yield the highly orderly systems that we find in the universe. It is a long story that science has yet to complete in detail. The point is that we see that this is one way to explain the development of the order.

An explanation saying that the order implements a creator's plan also works. We understand that machine-like order could have come about by implementing an intelligent design. P₂e says that the latter explanation is best. But so far, the two explanations seem equally capable of explaining the phenomenon in question. So why think that the latter one is better?

It is sometimes complained that the purely physical explanation just takes for granted that the physical laws and materials that exist produce the observed order. 'Yes,' it might be conceded, 'we can understand the presence of order, given the presence of physical laws and materials that just happen to go together to produce it. But this only pushes back the phenomenon requiring explanation: why is there this remarkable combination of physical materials and laws that mesh together so as to produce the observed high level of organization?'

Notice what this reply concedes. It acknowledges that the physical account explains the existence of the order. The complaint is that the physical account relies on something else, the combination of laws and the arrangement of materials, and they call for explanation.

This does not show that the physical explanation is worse than the explanation by design. The designing creator explanation relies on things too. It relies on the existence of an intelligent designer's plan for the universe to be as it is, and the designer's capacity to implement that plan in the universe. The existence of these things could use explaining too. It would be arbitrary simply to rest content with no explanation of them.

It is far from clear which explanation is in better shape here. A powerful intelligent being who planned and created the whole universe would be the most amazing thing in the world. Such a being can seem much *more* remarkable than the existence of natural laws and materials that happen to work together to generate the observed order. After all, we acknowledged some possibility of natural things just happening to produce a high degree of order, however unlikely it was. Is a designing creator even *that* likely? If the existence of the right physical ingredients calls for explanation, then the existence of a designing creator cries out for explanation.

Some have claimed that God's existence is self-explanatory; others have denied that it requires explanation. These claims are seriously obscure and doubtful. The first one seems to say that God exists because God exists—??? It never explains anything just to repeat what needs explaining. An all-powerful God would have what it takes to sustain a *continued* existence, if God exists. But God's existence in the first place is what we are concerned about now. Similarly, it is baffling to be told that God's existence requires no explanation. Why not? And if some reason can be given, why doesn't that reason also apply to the laws and materials of the physical account? Why do they still need explaining?

If there is anything finally better about the design explanation, it remains to be seen. Until it is definitely seen, P2e stands in doubt.

What about P1? Is the universe really so well organized all over the place? This is not clear. On the largest spatial scale that we currently observe, the galaxies are not randomly distributed. They tend to cluster. But that's it. They are not arrayed in some pinwheel pattern or any other fancy structure. As examples of organization, clusters are not impressive. Similarly, on the smallest spatial scale that we currently have information about, the scale of particles composed of quarks, we have trios of quarks bound closely together and jiggling about. That is not much like a complicated machine. When we look far back and far forward in time, the leading current cosmological views find considerably less intricate organization than is present today. Going far back toward the Big Bang, the theories say that things become ever less machine-like in structure. Going far forward toward the Big Chill, the theories say the same thing. So P1 is open to question.

We could replace P1 with a premise about the more localized order that is more clearly present in the world. But the smaller the portion of reality that displays machine-like order, the more probable it is that the order is accidental. Recall that our observations of accidents allow occasional patterns to be purely accidental effects of natural laws in operation. Does the extent of machine-like order in the whole world, throughout all of space and time, rise above that level? This is a question of detailed fact with no obvious answer.

There are other kinds of order that are sometimes cited in design arguments. One kind is the order that consists in the unbroken regularity of the operation of *natural laws*. This order is present throughout the known universe, including regions where machine-like structure is absent. If we replace P1 with a claim about the existence of this lawful order, does that make a better case for a designing creator?

The second premise will have to be adjusted too. It will have to claim that intelligent design best explains this lawful order. This new premise is open to doubt. When it comes to machine-like order, we are familiar with how minds introduce it. We have observed minds producing machines. But when it comes to something as perfectly uniform as the operation of a natural law, we have not observed minds implementing any such thing. Natural laws are like rules. Minds do invent rules. But intelligent minds in our experience do not enforce the same rules with no variation, ever, no matter what. Attributing such order to an intelligent design does not enable us to understand why the order exists, at least until we see a good enough reason for the absolute constancy.

This is an initial ground for doubt. Some views about God offer candidate reasons for God to institute unvarying laws. Also, according to some religious views natural laws are not perfectly constant, since they have been miraculously violated. These views in turn are disputed.

Another sort of order that some people point to as evidence of design is a kind of fine-tuning among physical magnitudes. According to current theories, if certain basic physical magnitudes had not been almost exactly the quantities that they are, they would have disallowed the development of complex atoms, much less human life. Does this argue that the universe was designed for us to exist in it?

Again, there is some ground for doubt. Suppose that human life depends on some exactly appropriate basic magnitudes in nature. Still, human life occupies an extremely small fraction of the known universe and it is extremely recent by cosmological standards. If the universe was designed for us by a mind intelligent and powerful enough to adjust physical magnitudes so that we would eventually get here, why didn't the mind produce us more efficiently?

Again, the initial doubt may be answerable. Perhaps the huge lifeless portion of space and time serves other intelligent purposes. Such purposes have been proposed, and disputed.

This issue will not be resolved here. There is no brief way to decide the merits of replacing our first premise with one about these other sorts of order. However the best version of the first premise finally works out, Phase 2 of the Design arguments has a problem that deserves our attention.

The doubts that were just raised about explanations by design are similar in spirit to some of David Hume's ideas in his wonderful work, *Dialogues Concerning Natural Religion*. P3 in Phase 2 is subject to some of Hume's powerful points. Hume suggests that we make use of *more specific details* in our observations of the origins of order. For instance, any large building project in our experience has multiple designers who have limited knowledge and ability. The universe was the largest building project of them all, if it was created by design. So our experience would lead us to expect a huge team of limited designers for such a project, rather than one all-knowing all-powerful God. Do we know anything else that overrides this lesson of experience? If not, then P3 is highly questionable.

Conceptually Guaranteeing God

A **concept** is a way of classifying something in our thinking. All of us have approximately a zillion concepts. We have the concept of a mammal, the concept of molasses, the concept of a toy, the concept of friendship, the concept of gravity, the concept of eyesight, the concept of danger, the concept of a boringly long list, and so on. A **singular concept** is a classification that brings to mind a single thing, if the concept applies at all. Singular concepts are entirely familiar. Examples from ordinary life abound. When Donna's daschund Dobson is in Donna's house alone, he is fond of luxuriating on the sofa, occupying his chosen pillow in regal comfort. While Dobson is doing this, we can bring him to mind in many ways—for example, by conceiving of him as the pooch on the couch, as the daschund on the pillow, and as the dog in the house. These are singular concepts that apply to Dobson.

One important line of thinking has it that God is the greatest being that anyone could bring to mind. If so, then one singular concept of God is the concept of the greatest conceivable being. We'll need the phrase 'greatest conceivable being' a lot. Let's abbreviate it with its initials: GCB.

Almost a thousand years ago the medieval philosopher Anselm argued that the GCB concept has to apply to an existing entity who is God, because of facts that we can discover by appreciating the nature of the concept itself. The reasoning is called 'Anselm's ontological argument'.[1] In one version or another, ontological arguments are particularly appealing to many philosophers. This appeal has something to do with the remarkable fact that we are supposed to be able to find out, just by thinking correctly, all that we need to know to see them prove their point. They are pure philosophy with a powerful payoff—*if* they work. The ontological argument that we'll consider is a reconstruction of Anselm's highly influential reasoning.

It'll be helpful to have a label for what a singular concept singles out. In other words, we want a term for the entity that meets the specifications of the concept, if anything does. The concept of Donna's dog, for instance, calls for a dog that is the

---

[1] The aim of this chapter in considering Anselm's argument is to think about whether it shows that God *actually* exists. In the chapter 'Why Not Nothing?' two other ontological arguments are discussed. The aim there is to determine whether they can show that a *necessary* being exists, whether or not the being qualifies as God.

cue owned by Donna. The concept applies to such a dog, or it does not apply. Let's label the entity that is singled out by a singular concept the **target** of the concept.

Typical singular concepts need not have a target. Consider the concept of the spoon on the moon. If a single spoon happens to be on the moon—maybe an astronaut left one there—then this concept has that spoon as its target. Otherwise the concept of the spoon on the moon has no target. Either way, the concept of the spoon on the moon is one of our concepts. The same goes for the singular concept of the pooch on the couch, the singular concept of the farthest star from the Earth, and so forth.

Key question: could our GCB concept lack a target?

No, according to Anselm. He asks us to suppose that the GCB concept has no target. In other words, suppose that the GCB does not exist. Anselm argues that if this were so, then we could form another concept that would be a concept of something *greater* than the GCB. Starting with our GCB concept, we can add the idea of existing. This gives us the concept of the *existing* GCB (the **EGCB** for short). Anselm holds that under circumstances where no GCB existed, our EGCB concept would be the concept of something greater than the GCB. The reason is that existing is a better status than not existing and we would be explicitly requiring existence in our EGCB concept.

But wait! Anselm points out that there is no possible way for us to form a concept of any being that is greater than the greatest conceivable one. The GCB is the greatest being that we can conceive of—it says so right in the concept itself. Therefore we cannot conceive of a greater being. Yet in the situation just described, we are supposed to be conceiving of a greater being. Since this is impossible, as we just saw, we must have assumed something untrue in setting up the situation. Anselm holds that the only questionable assumption in the setup is the initial one, the assumption that the GCB concept does not have a target. If that assumption is the mistake, then the GCB concept *does* apply to something. So the target of the GCB concept, the GCB, exists. The GCB is God. So God exists.

This reasoning can be summarized as follows.

Anselm's Ontological Argument

Phase 1

> *Temporary Assumption*: The GCB concept has no target.

Now add this premise:

> *Premise1:* If the GCB concept has no target, then the EGCB concept is a concept of something greater than the GCB concept.

From TA and P1, infer:

> *Temporary Conclusion*: The EGCB concept is a concept of something greater than the GCB concept.

Add another premise:

> *Premise2:* No concept is a concept of something greater than the GCB concept.

Premise2 says that TC is untrue, so the temporary assumption TA that got us TC must be false. In other words, infer:

> *Conclusion1:* The GCB concept does have a target.

Phase 2

> *Conclusion1:* The GCB concept does have a target.
> *Premise3:* If the GCB concept does have a target, then the GCB exists.
> *Conclusion2:* The GCB exists.

Phase 3

> *Conclusion2:* The GCB exists.
> *Premise4:* The GCB is God.
> *Conclusion3:* God exists.

Let's start our critical consideration of this argument on a positive note by contemplating P3. It is entirely okay. If a singular concept has a target, then the concept does apply to some existing thing. For example, since the singular concept of Donna's dog has Dobson as a target, Donna's dog exists.

Now let's consider the final assumption, P4. It seems pretty credible at first. But maybe we can conceive of something greater than God. Such as? Well, consider someone with limited abilities who overcomes adversity and acts heroically. In a way, such a person seems to be better than any being of unlimited power and knowledge who is morally flawless. That sort of being is too knowledgeable and powerful to be heroic. Maybe heroism is one feature of a conceivable being who would be overall greater than a being who has the power and knowledge of the traditional God.

This is debatable. God could still turn out to be the greatest. For instance, the greatness of God might consist in God's having all of the important positive properties, like knowledge, ability, and moral goodness, to a *maximum* extent. That sounds like an unbeatable combination.

This idea that God has the maximum degree of greatness is a risky one, though. The important positive properties may not all have a *possible* maximum. For example, part of being morally good is doing good. Yet no matter how much good someone does, it seems *possible* to have done more good. So moral goodness may not have a maximum. If not, then we don't get the GCB by conceiving of a being who is *maximally* morally good, because we get an impossible being. Any being that does exist and is good surely outdoes the greatness of any impossible being. Thus, the maximum idea of God is a problematic way to try to establish God as the GCB.

Much more thinking is needed to draw a justified conclusion about the truth of P4. But regardless of how well Phase 3 with P4 works out, successful reasoning through Phase 2 would be nothing to sneeze at. A proof of Phase 2's conclusion, C2, would be mighty metaphysically interesting. Establishing the actual existence of the greatest conceivable being would show us something wonderful about reality.

P1 and P2 are taken for granted in Phase 1. If either one of them is untrue, then C1 is not proven in Phase 1. Without success in Phase 1, the whole argument collapses. Let's think more about P1.

P1 says that if the GCB concept has no target, then the EGCB concept is 'of' something greater. The interpretation of the small word 'of' turns out to be crucial to assessing the argument. Two interpretations should be distinguished. First, for a concept to be 'of' a greater being, on one interpretation, is for a greater being to be the concept's target. This interpretation gives us:

> P1i: If the GCB concept has no target, then the target of the EGCB concept is a greater thing than the target of the GCB concept.

If the GCB concept has no target, then it is easy for *some* other concept to have a greater target. The other concept would just have to apply to something that is greater than nothing. Again, anything good is greater than nothing. So a concept of a good thing that exists would qualify as having a greater target than the GCB concept. But would the EGCB concept in particular have a greater target, as P1i says?

Suppose that the GCB concept has no target. Recall that this means that the GCB concept does not apply to anything. If nothing is the greatest conceivable being, then nothing is the *existing* greatest conceivable being either. Thus, if the one concept applies to nothing, then so does the other. Since they both lack targets, the greatness of their targets is the greatness of nothing—worthless! Therefore, if the GCB concept has no target, then GCB concept and the EGCB concept would be tied at zero for the greatness of their targets. This denies the P1i claim that the EGCB concept would have a *greater* target. So if we have interpreted P1 correctly as P1i, then it is untrue.

There is another interpretation of P_1. The new idea is that if the GCB concept has no target, then the EGCB concept demands more greatness than does the GCB concept. In other words, if no GCB exists, then in the competition for being our way of conceiving of the greatest being that we can possibly conceive of, the EGCB concept would beat out the GCB concept. Both concepts clearly require extreme greatness to apply. But according to P1 as we are now interpreting it, in the absence of a real GCB, the EGCB concept would require the greater greatness. This gives us:

> P1ii: If the GCB concept has no target, then the greatness needed for the EGCB concept to apply is more than the greatness needed for the GCB concept to apply.

P1ii does not stand scrutiny. The GCB concept goes all out in its demand for greatness—it demands 'the greatest'. It *demands* maximal greatness, whether or not its demand is *met*. For example, existing appears to be part of what it takes to be the greatest thing that we can conceive of. Any 'things' that could have existed, but don't exist, at most *could have been* great. 'They' aren't great. 'They' aren't anything, much less anything great. If this appearance that existence is needed for greatness is correct, then the GCB concept demands existence just as much as the EGCB concept. If this appearance is incorrect, then the EGCB concept does not demand more greatness by explicitly demanding existence.

There is just no way for the GCB concept to be beaten in this competition. The GCB concept requires 'the greatest', and that's that! Yet P1ii alleges that under one particular condition—the nonexistence of the GCB—the EGCB concept demands more greatness. We have just seen that it couldn't, though. So this other interpretation of P1 is untrue and does not help Anselm's ontological argument. Phase 1 of the argument relies on the truth of some interpretation of P1. Since the argument needs

Phase 1 to work in order to get anywhere, the argument goes nowhere if our criticism is correct.

Putting it All Together

We have found problems in each of the arguments for God's existence that we have considered. Let's not leap to any conclusions. Even if we had found problems in *all* arguments for God's existence, it would not follow that God does not exist. Entities whose existence cannot be proven by us might exist. They might exist without being in any revealing sort of relation to us. God could be like that. Or God could be revealed by an argument that we have not considered.

Let's not leap away from any conclusions either, though. The arguments that we have seen for God's existence do not work.

Sometimes each clue to a crime on its own does not mean much, while together they argue powerfully for a certain culprit. Likewise, the thoughts from several arguments might work better in combination. The most reasonable belief that we can have about something is one based on *all* relevant available evidence. So before we draw any conclusive conclusions about God's existence, we would do best to look at the combined strength of our arguments.

There are initial indications of an improved case. For instance, it seems to become more reasonable to think that the universe had God as first cause when we add in the observations from our discussion of the design argument that support the idea that the universe displays various sorts of order. On the other hand, the doubts raised about whether the universe really is organized as though by an intelligent designer carry over as doubts that God was its first cause.

Assessing the strength of a combined case for God's existence would require assessing together everything in the First Cause and Design arguments, and the Ontological argument as well. Having done this, we would still not be in a position to draw the most rational conclusion. More evidence exists. There are other arguments for God's existence. There are arguments against God's existence too. The most prominent one—the **Problem of Evil**—contends that an all-powerful, all-knowing, morally perfect being would never allow all of the bad things that exist in this world, and so no such being exists. Several versions of this argument have been developed. They have in turn received intense critical scrutiny. All of that is more of the evidence available on the topic of God's existence. And then there's the challenge of assembling and weighing the totality of the evidence . . . We never said that metaphysics was quick and easy!

There's no need to get discouraged, either. With our consideration of the central metaphysical arguments, a serious investigation of God's existence is well under way.

FURTHER READING

Philosophy on the topic of God's existence comprises a huge literature. Here are two significant recent books. The first one is favorably disposed toward arguments against the existence of God; the second one is favorably disposed toward arguments for the existence of God.

Jordan Howard Sobel, *Logic and Theism* (Cambridge University Press, 2004).

Richard Swinburne, *The Existence of God, 2nd edn*. (Oxford University Press, 2004).

CHAPTER 5

Why Not Nothing?

Earl Conee

Introduction

Suppose that you find pickles in your potato soup. You ask indignantly, 'Why are there pickles in my potato soup?' You are told that Mort put them in when he prepared your soup. He did so because good old Bob told him, as a prank, that you favor pickles in your potato soup.

You may well remain dissatisfied, but the presence of the pickles has been explained to you. It is not an exhaustive explanation. It takes much for granted. It doesn't explain Bob's desire to play a prank or Mort's capacity to make soup. More fundamentally, it doesn't explain the existence of Mort, Bob, or the pickles. A fuller explanation would explain those things. It too would take a lot for granted, though, probably including some background conditions and general principles of psychology and biology.

The explanatory structure of this example seems to be completely typical. Seemingly, any answer to any question has to take something for granted. Explanations use some things to explain others.

But then there is the following metaphysical question, where taking anything for granted appears to be disallowed. Also, it seems to be as basic as a question can get.

Q: Why is there something, rather than nothing?

Q asks why there is anything at all. Any answer to Q that is based on something seems to be immediately disqualified. Whatever the basis for the answer, Q asks for an explanation of why that basis exists in the first place. Yet how could an answer be any good if it is not based on anything?

What is the Question?

We should be sure that we are focusing on a metaphysical question. We should set aside nearby scientific ones. According to established science, the whole universe emerged from an explosion, the Big Bang. If so, then one question we can ask is this:

QBB: What explains the Big Bang—why did it happen?

There is no established scientific answer to QBB. But it is a scientific issue. An answer might give a typical sort of causal explanation of the Big Bang. Such an explanation would identify one or more events and conditions that made the Big Bang happen in accordance with natural law. Or an answer might use just natural laws. It might be discovered that one or more basic laws of nature entail that the Big Bang was inevitable, or that it was more or less probable.

In any case, with a little further thought we'll see that Q definitely does not ask for an explanation of the Big Bang that cites causes or laws. In fact, the main question that Q seems to be asking looks altogether unanswerable.

To clarify the metaphysical question, let's consider the most minimal alternative reality that we can specify. This is an absolutely empty reality—no material objects, no dimensions of space or time, just nothing. And by 'nothing' here we truly mean: nothing! Our maximally minimal reality does not include any objects or dimensions; it does not include any natural laws or any tendencies. It is empty in every way. Let's call it 'W'.

This W at least appears to have been a possible alternative to the actual situation. One question that Q can ask is the following one:

QM: Why there is anything more to reality than W?

If QM is what Q asks, then scientific replies to the question about the Big Bang—in terms of causes or laws—seem disqualified. Those replies tell us why something happened, namely, the Big Bang, by relying on at least one other thing that explains its occurrence, such as a cause or a law. But QM asks about the existence of those other things too, since W includes none of them. QM asks why anything exists of any sort at all. So it seems that an answer to this question cannot take for granted the existence of any sort of thing, not even a natural law. All answers available from science seem to take for granted at least one such entity without explaining why it exists.

Do we Get the Question?

Do we really understand QM? After all, we have no familiarity with the phenomenon of there being nothing at all. In fact, calling it a 'phenomenon' is an overstatement. Nothingness is the absence of all phenomena, and everything else. The mind boggles.

On second thought, though, the mind doesn't stay boggled. Let's start with the word 'nothing'. A reality in which nothing exists is just a reality in which there isn't anything—no thing of any kind. We get that idea. We cannot *imagine* it. A silent blank void is as close as we can come, and that is not nothing. It is a spatial region with no sound, light, or matter. That is something. But understanding a topic of a question does not require being able to imagine that topic. For instance, we can understand questions that are about amazement. We have a good idea of what amazement is. Yet we have no mental image of amazement. We can imagine, say, Amanda's being amazed. But that is only an image of Amanda making some typical display of amazement. It is not an image of the psychological state of amazement itself. Likewise, we have some understanding of what possibility is. We can picture specific possible things, but not their possibility. Yet we do not have a problem with understanding the topics of amazement and possibility well enough to comprehend questions about those topics. So if there is a problem understanding what QM is asking, it is not that we cannot imagine what it is about.

More positively, here is a reason to think that we do understand the question. We understand each word in QM. The word 'why' comes closest to making trouble. This is not because we draw a blank. It is just that we lack full clarity about it. The 'why' asks for explanation. Explanations differ. The question does not specify what sort of explanation is sought. In any case, we do see that it asks for an explanation. This is enough to make sense of the question. In addition to understanding the words in QM separately, we also see how they relate grammatically. We can put them together and comprehend the whole thing. We can show our understanding by rephrasing QM with four easy words: why is there anything? We do get the question.

To say that we understand a question is not to suggest that the question is easy to investigate, much less to answer. In the case of QM, it is not even easy to say what would qualify as an answer. In fact, answering QM seems hopeless, at least at first. How could there be an explanation that does not rely on anything?

Necessitarianism

Perhaps all explanations do rely on something. According to one important tradition on this topic, though, that fact does not prevent us from solving the problem posed by Q. The tradition says that we can explain why the possible reality that actually exists has something in it, unlike the maximally empty W, by showing that W is not even possible. We can understand why there is something rather than nothing, by seeing that there *has to be* something. More specifically, we can be shown that one or more particular somethings have to exist. These would be **necessary beings**, that is, beings that exist in any and all possible situations. By seeing why one or more necessary beings exist, we understand why there is actually something. We understand that this turns out to have been inevitable.

Suppose that we can also see that each thing relied on to establish the existence of some necessary being is itself a necessary being. If so, then we do not have to worry about the fact that we are relying on things to explain things. If we really can see that they are all inevitable, then we are left with no reason to wonder why they actually exist.

This necessitarian approach sounds promising in form, but it is dubious in substance. If it is correct, then we were making a mistake in thinking of the totally thing-free W as a possibility. Yet exactly what would be impossible about W? Just that it lacks objects? But how could that be impossible? Temporary emptiness of some spatial region is possible. Once we grant this, there seems to be no upper limit on how much space can be empty and for how long. So why not a whole empty reality? Is W impossible because it lacks all natural laws? But what could be inevitable about laws of nature? Some things could have happened by chance rather than by law. Why couldn't reality have been entirely lawless? And if some possible reality with objects and events in it is lawless, then why would there have to be natural laws if there were no objects? So again, just what is impossible about W?

Godly Necessitarianism

Necessitarians have answers to these questions. There is a major division in necessitarian approaches at this point between theological necessitarians and nontheological ones. According to one main theological view, God is a necessary being. God would exist under any possible circumstances. So there could not have been nothing.

We should note an initial doubt about Godly necessitarianism. It is subject to a problem of vanishing possibilities. We are talking about the traditional God here. God has to be the all-knowing, all-powerful, perfectly loving, and benevolent creator of the universe. Apparent possibilities vanish when we ask what sort of a reality such a being would allow to exist. For instance, it seems clear that there are some evils that God would not allow—perhaps the existence of suffering for no good reason, or the existence of unjustified human degradation. So, if the traditional God is a necessary being, such evil is not possible. The appearance that the evil was even possible would be an illusion. Yet we can spell out in as much detail as we like how things go in a reality that includes such evils but not God. Leaving God out of the situation does not give any appearance of making it an impossibility. So its impossibility is dubious.

And that is not all. Would God allow a reality in which there was no sentient life? Seemingly not. Seemingly, a perfectly loving and benevolent being would want to share existence with sentient creatures, and have those creatures do very well in their lives. An all-powerful being would be able to create thriving sentient beings. So no possible reality would be without them, if God exists necessarily. Thus, many more apparent possibilities would turn out to be merely apparent.

Note that the *existence* of God does not make this trouble. It can be that God actually exists. As long as God is not a necessary being, worthless and repugnant possibilities do not have to be allowed by God in order for them to be possible. It can be that God is not in those alternative realities to prevent such inexcusably miserable things. It is the assumption of a *necessary* God that gives rise to the problem of vanishing possibilities. That is the very assumption of interest to us here, though, since it is the assumption that implies that there could not have been nothing.

The problem gets worse. Apparently, any flaw or defect of any kind would be avoidable, with no net cost, by one who had sufficient knowledge and power. A being with boundless love, power, and benevolence would avoid all defects. So it seems that wherever such a being exists, the world would be entirely lacking in defects. And the same goes for any other imperfection—it would be banished. If this is correct, then only perfection is even possible, if God is necessary. Yet that seems to leave out virtually all of the possibilities! Almost everything that we would otherwise have thought to be possible is less than perfect. All of that would turn out to be impossible. Amazing! Thus, there seems to be a high price in credibility to pay for thinking that God is a necessary being. So why think so?

Ontological Arguments for a Necessary Being

Let's look into a classic sort of argument for a necessary God, an ontological argument.[1] Our initial version of it will have two

---

[1] The ontological arguments in this chapter aim to prove the necessary existence of a being who is traditionally identified as God. The ontological argument of the 'God' chapter aims to prove the actual existence of God. Both

phases. The first assumption of the first phase is the claim that the concept of God is the concept of a being who is maximally perfect. If that is not your concept of God, it does not matter for present purposes. We are looking for a necessary being to answer our present question. If the necessary being happens to fit your concept of God, or otherwise qualify as God, then that is an additionally interesting and important fact. But it is actually incidental to present purposes.[2] We will not even use the term 'God' in our formulation of the argument. The current argument aims to establish the existence of a necessary being by using the concept of the most perfect being. We can scrutinize the merits of this reasoning, whatever the connection turns out to be between the most perfect being and other understandings of God.

Let's begin with a preliminary sketch of the argument. It is about a concept. **Concepts** are our ideas; they are our ways of thinking about things. The first assumption of our first version of the argument asserts the existence of a particular concept. It says that there is a concept of something that is maximally perfect. The other assumption of the first phase of the argument is that it is impossible for anything to be maximally perfect without existing. Relying on these assumptions, the first phase concludes that something that is maximally perfect exists.

The second phase of the argument adds the third and final assumption. This is where necessary existence comes in. The claim of the final assumption is that necessary existence is implied by maximal perfection. Using this assumption together with the conclusion of the first phase, the argument draws the final conclusion: something maximally perfect exists necessarily (!).

Here is the whole thing in a nutshell.

versions to be discussed in this chapter derive primarily from Rene Descartes's presentations of the argument in his *Meditations* and *Replies to Caterus*, though they are not primarily intended to be historically faithful renditions of his reasoning. The first version owes most to the *Meditations*.

[2] The focus is reversed in the chapter 'God'.

First Ontological Argument

Phase 1

> *Premise1*: There is a concept of something that is maximally perfect
>
> *Premise2*: Anything that is maximally perfect must exist.
>
> *Conclusion1*: Something that is maximally perfect exists.

Phase 2

> *Conclusion1*: Something that is maximally perfect exists.
>
> *Premise3*: Anything that is maximally perfect exists necessarily.
>
> *Conclusion2*: Something maximally perfect exists necessarily.

If this argument succeeds, then our hypothetical entirely empty alternative reality W turns out to be impossible. A perfect being has to exist, no matter what.

This argument has strengths. Initially, Premise1 ('P1' for short) looks safe. We do have that *concept* at least, don't we? Well, we'll see . . . Meanwhile, the claim of P2 seems even safer. Doesn't a thing have to exist, in order to be maximally perfect? After all, doesn't a thing have to exist, just in order to be pretty good, or mediocre, or even bad, much less perfect?

Actually, this has been doubted. For instance, isn't it a fact that Santa Claus is a very good fellow, distributing all of those presents every year? Yet Santa does not exist. So existence is not required in order to be good.

On reflection, though, that reasoning looks faulty. It is not really so that Santa is good, period. And this is not because of any scandalous hidden truth establishing that Santa is bad. It is just that no Santa exists to be in any condition at all, good, bad, or otherwise. Rather, the fact in the vicinity is just that, *according to the Santa folklore*, Santa is good. This fact does not imply that Santa is actually good, any more than it implies that Santa exists.

Anyway, P2 is defensible even if some fictional character manages to be good without existing. P2 says that to be *maximally* perfect, a thing must exist. Maybe unreal things like Santa can be good, maybe even perfect in some ways. As long as the uppermost level of perfection is reserved for existing things, that is all the second assumption says. And that is plausible. Unreal things, however glorious in their own way, are rather ethereal and inconsequential in comparison to anything great that actually exists.

P3 is also plausible. It is easy to believe that necessary existence is in some way better than contingent existence. Necessary existence is definitely more impressive. Perhaps this is because necessary existence has a special sort of perfection not shared by contingent existence.

But let's reconsider the initial assumption, P_1, which says that there is a concept of something that is maximally perfect. Again, this initially seems beyond doubt. We can just consult our inventory of concepts and, sure enough, we have the concept of something maximally perfect. Doesn't that settle the existence of a concept of something maximally perfect?

Yes and no. The meaning of P_1 turns on how we take the ambiguous word 'of' in its wording. Here is an analogous case with the same ambiguity. Suppose I say, 'There is a painting of an animal on my wall.' This sentence is ambiguous—what I say might be true in two drastically different ways. First, it might be that a painting on my wall is 'of' an animal, because it is a portrait of a particular animal, say, a certain moose that the artist saw. Using 'of' in this way, our claim attributes a relationship between two existing things: the canvas on my wall and that moose. The claim says that the one portrays the other in paint.

But equally, it might be that I have a painting 'of' an animal by having on the wall a painting that represents a mythical animal, say, a hippogriff. It is still correctly called a painting 'of' an animal, but now in a new sense. Hippogriffs do not exist. No actual animal was painted. The new meaning is that it would take a certain sort of animal for the painting to portray something real. In effect, the painting specifies how part of the world would have to be for the painting to have been drawn from life. It would take the existence of a hippogriff for the painting to be an accurate depiction of something. When a painting requires an animal in this way—in order to be drawn from life—that is something else that we call a painting 'of' an animal.

The same goes for concepts. You do not have a concept 'of' something as being maximally perfect, understanding 'of' in the first way, unless you are related to some existing thing by conceiving it to be maximally perfect. The two of you have to exist and you have to be conceptually related to it. In contrast, you have a concept 'of' something as maximally perfect, understanding 'of' in the second way, if you have a concept that applies to something only if that something is maximally perfect. The concept specifies a standard. It calls for the utmost perfection. Unless that level of perfection is there, the concept does not apply. But the concept can exist and specify maximal perfection in order to apply, without actually applying. We still say that it is the concept 'of' something maximally perfect. We say this to signify that the concept requires maximal perfection for it to apply, just as something can be a painting 'of' a hippogriff because the painting requires an actual hippogriff to be an accurate depiction.

Equipped with this distinction, we can interpret P1. P1 says that there is a concept 'of' something that is maximally perfect. Is that true? Well, if we take the 'of' in the second way, then there is such a concept. We do have the idea of being maximally perfect. At least, we have this idea abstractly, however unsure we may be about details of what makes for the highest level of perfection. We have the idea of something having whatever it takes to be most perfect. So we must agree that this concept exists. Interpreted in this way, P1 is true.

But now comes trouble for the argument. When we combine this interpretation of P1 with P2, the conclusion of the first phase does not follow. P2 says: anything that *is* maximally perfect must exist. So, in order for P2 to help to imply the first phase conclusion, namely, that a maximally perfect being exists, P2 has to work in combination with a claim to the effect that something *is* maximally perfect. Yet P1 now does not say that anything is maximally perfect. P1 says only that a concept exists that has maximal perfection as a requirement for its application. P1 does not imply that this requirement is met. Thus, when we understand the 'of' in P1 in this way, Phase 1 of the argument goes wrong.

Understanding 'of' in P1 the other way makes one large improvement. The conclusion of the first phase now follows. P1 now says all of this: there is a concept and there is a something, these two are related in such a way that the first is a concept of the second, and the second is maximally perfect. So now P1 implies that something *is* maximally perfect. Thus, since P2 says that whatever is maximally perfect must exist, it follows that something maximally perfect does exist, just as the conclusion says.

Taking P1 in this way, with the 'of' relating a concept to an existing thing, why believe it? Only this much is clear: there is a concept that applies to something that is maximally perfect, *if it applies at all*. When we had P1 saying *only* that much, though, we were back with the other interpretation and its problem. The argument needs P1 to claim something beyond that. It needs P1 to claim that there is something to which the maximal perfection concept *does* apply. So *we* need a good answer to the question: why believe that it applies? If we already knew that a most perfect thing existed, then we could use that knowledge to justify this claim about the concept applying. But we don't already know that. It is what we're trying to see proven. Without knowing that, we lack justification for believing the claim that the concept applies. So P1 stands in need of justification. An argument with an unjustified assumption does not prove anything.

Thus, either way we read the 'of' in the first assumption, this version of the ontological argument for a necessary being appears to fail in its first step.

In our quest for a necessitarian answer to Q, we seek something that exists necessarily. In the version of the Ontological argument that we just considered, the inference to necessary existence occurs in the second phase. We have seen that the reasoning gets into trouble before that. So we didn't even get to anything about necessary existence. We should briefly look at a version that involves necessary existence from the beginning.[3]

The new version begins by assuming that the 'essential nature' of the maximally perfect being includes existing necessarily. Something's **essential nature** is the combination of features that the thing has to have in order to exist. Therefore, whatever features we discover in a thing's essential nature must characterize it, no matter what its circumstances are—including its actual circumstances. Again, the assumption says that necessary existence is one of the features in the essential nature of the maximally perfect being.

The other assumption in the new version spells out an inescapable connection between a feature being in a thing's essential nature and the thing's having that feature. The assumption is that if necessary existence is included in something's nature, then the thing exists necessarily. These two premises yield the conclusion that the maximally perfect being exists necessarily.

---

[3] This second version is suggested by some of what Descartes says in his *Replies to Caterus*.

Premise1: The essential nature of the maximally perfect being includes existing necessarily.

Premise2: If necessary existence is included in the essential nature that some being has, then the being exists necessarily.

Conclusion: The maximally perfect being exists necessarily.

One good thing about this version is that the second assumption, P2, is not seriously disputable. If a being has necessary existence in its nature, then that being has necessary existence—that's for sure.

Support for the new P1 derives from some thinking about perfection that is familiar to us. The supporting idea is that when we reflect on what goes into the loftiest heights of perfection, one feature that we find included is that of having the most impressive sort of existence, namely, necessary existence. That reflection seems to be the best defense of P1.

Trouble for our Second Ontological Argument is familiar too. The current P1 includes the phrase 'the essential nature *of* the maximally perfect being'. There is that 'of' again. On one reading, this phrase has the premise say, among other things, that the maximally perfect being exists and has a nature. If the first assumption says that, then it ruins the argument. The argument is supposed to prove that a maximally perfect being exists. An argument cannot prove anything that it assumes to be true.

On the other hand, P1 may be just claiming something about a requirement for a concept to apply. P1 can be interpreted as saying that there is a concept that applies to a most perfect being, if at all, and in order for it to apply, the being must have an essential nature that includes necessary existence. All of that is plausible. It does not assume that a most perfect being exists. So let's read P2 that way.

Familiar trouble arises. Now the needed logical link to the conclusion has been lost. The second premise, P2, makes a claim about 'the essential nature that some being has'. So in order for P1 to link with the claim made by P2, P1 has to be about a being that *has* some nature. Yet as we now read P1, it does not say that anything has any nature. It just specifies a requirement for a concept to apply. So the two premises do not work together to imply the conclusion.

Thus, either way we read P_1, the reasoning fails to prove the existence of a necessary being. Let's try something else.

Ungodly Necessitarianism

A necessitarian answer to the question of why anything exists does not require anything as exalted and wonderful as a maximally perfect thing. Any necessary being of any sort, however otherwise unexciting, would fill the bill. The entirely empty reality W would turn out to be impossible. There are numerous humbler candidates for the status of necessary being.

Let's use the label 'W*' for a definitely *possible* reality that is as empty as it is possible to be. *If* it is possible for there to be nothing at all, then W* is identical to W. But if more is needed for W* to have been a genuine possibility, then W* includes the least more that makes it possible. The following is a new necessitarian reason to think that W* must contain something, and so W is not possible.

How would things be in W*? 'Things' may be the wrong word, because there is as close as possible to nothing in W*. But still, there is a factual situation in W*. It is a fact about W* that it is as empty as can be, for instance. We should rephrase our question. What would be true in W*? Well, for instance, W* would lack all moose, since no moose is a necessary being. It seems to follow that it would be true in W* that there are no moose.

Aren't truths something, though? For instance, it is an actual truth *that there are moose*. In saying this, it seems that we are referring to an entity that *is* that particular truth. The standard philosopher's term for this sort of thing is **proposition**. If we state that there are moose, a proposition is what we state; if we believe that there are moose, the same proposition is what we believe. Any truth is a proposition. And since the proposition that there are moose is a truth, it exists. In general, in order to be in any condition at all, an entity has to exist. In some other possible realities, in W^* for instance, that proposition is another way. It is false in W^*, because there are no moose there. Since the proposition is in the condition of being false there, the proposition exists there. Any proposition is either true or false about any possible conditions. So if we take this line about propositions, we can conclude that any proposition is a necessary being.

Thus, the minimal possible reality W^* is *not* the absolutely empty W, because W^* has propositions in it. The general necessitarian answer to the question of why reality is not absolutely empty is that some things have to exist. The present version of necessitarianism says specifically that there have to exist the truths of each possible reality, and the falsehoods too.

Was it really legitimate to infer the existence in W^* of the proposition that there are no moose? There would have been no moose, were W^* to have been the real world. That is actually true, and it is about W^*. So it might follow that this proposition *actually* exists. But why does the proposition that there are no moose, or any other proposition, have to exist *in W^* too*? There would be no moose in W^*, but how exactly does that imply that there would exist in W^* an entity that is the substance of the claim that there are no moose? We said that there is a factual situation in W^*. Maybe that is only loosely accurate. Maybe the strict truth is this. Here in the actual world, where we are reasoning about W^*, there do exist facts that are about how things would be in W^*. But, were W^* to have been the actual world, there would have been no factual situation. There would have been nothing, not even the truth that there was nothing. Why not think that W^* is the absolutely empty W after all?

Minimal Contingency

Whether or not there are any necessary beings, an important version of Q remains to be considered:

QC: Why is there anything that does not have to exist?

Our minimally occupied possible reality, W^*, includes necessary beings if there are any. But W^* includes nothing **contingent**. In other words, W^* includes nothing that exists without having to exist. Yet the actual situation is clearly populated by things that do not have to exist: moose, moons, muons, moors, and more. QC does not ask why *all* of the particular real things exist. (That is a good question, but a different one.) QC asks why any *unnecessary* thing exists. QC asks why there is any contingency, anything beyond the absolute minimum.

Anthropic Explanation

An anthropic explanation might seem helpful here. **Anthropic explanations** seek to account for some phenomenon by pointing out how the phenomenon is required in order for us to exist and thus to be in a position to investigate it. In the present instance, the idea would be something like this. Any possible reality must contain a multitude of contingent things, in order for us to exist in that reality and ask QC. At the very least, it must contain us. We are not necessary beings. So it is no wonder that the actual world has contingent things in it and is therefore not the minimally occupied W^*.

It is doubtful that this anthropic account answers QC satisfactorily. The account gives a good answer, but it is an answer to a different question. Suppose that we were asking this:

QWC: Why does the world in which we exist include contingent things?

QWC takes it for granted that we are in the world, and asks why contingent things are present with us. If that is something we wonder about, then it seems to be directly responsive to point out that we are contingent ourselves. That observation seems capable of removing any puzzlement about why a reality with us in it has contingencies.

Unlike QWC, QC does not ask about what accompanies us in the actual world. It is true that, if there were no contingent things, then we would not exist to ask QC. But QC asks about our existence as just as much as it asks about the existence of any other contingent thing. When we are asking QC, we are asking why any contingent thing at all actually exists. A reply that just identifies something that is required for us to exist is unresponsive to this question.

Godly Explanation

God might seem helpful in answering QC. If God is a necessary being, then God is in our minimal possible reality, W^*. We can assume that God has the power to create contingent things. It seems that God's reason for creating contingent things would explain why they exist too.

But we have also seen that a necessary God gives rise to a problem of vanishing possibilities. Here, the problem plays itself out as a difficulty about what contingencies God could create. First, perhaps under any possible circumstances God would have exactly the same reasons for creating, and God would use those reasons in the very same way to decide what to create. If so, then it seems that God would always create exactly the same reality. We are assuming that God is a necessary being. Given this, just one creation would be the only possible created reality. It would not even be contingent, since it would exist along with God in the one combination of circumstances that is even possible.

This is a problem, because it surely seems that there are many different contingent possibilities. For instance, there are actually various hummingbirds in various places. Had their habitats happened to develop differently, hummingbirds would have been more or less differently distributed. That gives every appearance of being a possibility. There are countless similar ones. It is difficult to believe that the seeming existence of multiple possibilities is entirely misleading.

Let's try something else. Suppose again that there is a necessary God. But now suppose that in different possible realities God has different reasons for creating. If so, then those differences allow for the different contingencies. There would be the different possible created outcomes, none of them necessary.

But then the initial differences in God's reasons would turn out to be the origin of the contingencies. All differences would stem from these variations in God's reasons. Assuming all of this, QC would turn out to be asking: why do any of these variations in God's reasons exist? To answer QC, we would need to explain why God has any particular batch of these reasons . . . ?

A third alternative does somewhat better. Perhaps God's reasons for creating leave ties among possible creations. That is, there might be alternative contingent realities that are exactly equally best at fulfilling all of God's purposes. The different possibilities arise from God's ability to choose freely from among these alternatives. In each different alternative reality, God makes a different free choice about which of these creations to bring about.

The main trouble with this new answer is that it can account for only a narrow range of possibilities. Recall that it is part of this explanation that God is a necessary being. So there is no possible reality without God. The possible creations by God as we are now understanding them drastically restrict the possibilities. In all possible realities God's reasons for creating are fulfilled. Yet many other things appear to have been possible. For example, all of the following seem possible: thoroughly boring mindless realities that would have been of no value by any standard, unfortunate realities where the bad outweighs the good, and fairly nice realities where most lives are worth living while none are terrific. It is not credible that these alternatives would flawlessly fulfill the reasons that a perfect God would have for creating. Thus, the free choices of a necessary God would reject all of these apparent possibilities. Such choices could explain only contingencies that would perfectly fulfill perfect purposes.

Since we recognize more possibilities than that, we have to keep looking for their explanation. On the other hand, if God is not necessary, then at best God is part of the present problem and not its solution. Wherever God does exist, God is one of the contingencies for which we seek an explanation by asking QC. And wherever God does not exist, God is not there to make any choices that might explain contingent things.

Tendentious Explanation

If not God, then what about goodness? Let's consider the idea that good things that can exist have an innate tendency to exist. The more perfect possible things have a greater tendency to exist than the less perfect. The better things are overall in a possible reality, the stronger is the tendency of that possibility to be actual.[4]

---

[4] Leibniz, one of the leading philosophers of the 17th century, proposed something along these lines.

Various things are credibly regarded as good, including benevolent deeds, pleasant experiences, beautiful art, and enriching relationships. When we survey the candidates for goodness, it becomes clear that all reasonable candidates involve the existence of contingent things like people and experiences. In contrast, it is clear that our maximally empty possible reality W^* is thoroughly neutral in value. W^* is too blank to be any good. In this view, then, W^* is just barely possible. It does not have the propensity to exist that better possibilities possess. Thus, the new explanation of why there is something beyond the contents of W^* is that the actual existence of contingent good things manifests the intrinsic tendency of possible good things to exist.

The idea that the good tends to exist is comforting. It has three problematic features, though. The least fundamental problem is that the idea seems unjustifiably optimistic. Why is it *good* things that have this tendency, rather than bad or neutral things? Of course any decent person finds the good more attractive than the other two, and so decent people are drawn to produce and preserve the good. But this cannot explain why there are any contingent things at all. The claim is that there is a tendency to exist that each possible good thing has on its own, without the assistance of appreciative people who already exist. The alleged tendency to exist of the good possibilities needs some defense.

That problem is not fundamental, because there is an equally satisfactory explanation of contingent things that lacks this bias toward the good. It could be claimed instead that all contingent things, good, bad, or indifferent, have a propensity to exist. This would provide the core of the same sort of explanation. Again, W^* is just barely possible, while the actual world displays countless manifestations of the tendency toward existence of contingent things.

A second and more basic problem with this idea is the obscurity of the relevant tendency. Our understanding of tendencies seems to require that they be possessed by existing things and explained by existing things. For instance, fragile things have a tendency to break. The breaking does not already exist and may never exist. Some fragile things never break. But all things that *have* this tendency do exist, and the tendency is accounted for by the structure and environment that those things actually have. A possessor of tendencies might be remarkably hollow. Current physics asserts a tendency for particles to form in empty space. But if so, this is a tendency of something actual, space, and it is explained by something actual, physical law. We are totally unfamiliar with a tendency that is had by something merely possible that does not exist.

This obscurity is part of a wider problem. Having a tendency to exist is having a certain feature. Yet the explanation attributes this feature to things that merely *might have existed*. It is difficult to make sense of mere possibilities having any features at all. We can understand how various specifications *would* specify things having certain features *if* those specifications were realized. We have a much harder time with the idea that some alleged entity, although it is no real thing, nonetheless manages to have the feature of tending to exist. *What* has the feature? An unreal thing? Isn't the phrase 'an unreal thing' like the phrase 'a fake duck'? Just as fake ducks are not ducks at all, unreal things are not things at all. There are no such things! And if there are no such things, then there are no such things to have any tendencies.

Even if we could make sense of the idea that some possible contingencies have a tendency to exist, there would remain a different sort of fundamental problem for the view. What reason do we have to think that any such tendency claim is true? Compare this claim that contingencies tend to exist with the opposite claim. It could be claimed that it is *difficult* to get into existence. It could be claimed that all contingent things are prone *not* to exist, while the 'easy emptiness' of W* had a strong tendency to be realized. This view would conclude that the actual world contains contingencies by a fluke. The existence of contingencies would run contrary to the tendency among possibilities.

This opposite hypothesis seems no less credible than the other one. The problematic fact for any tendency-style explanation is that we have no reason to believe in any such tendency.

Statistical Explanation

Here is a final idea about why there is anything real that does not have to exist. As we have repeatedly noted, it is plausible that diverse contingencies are possible. Some seemingly possible realities contain life and some do not; some are governed by laws of nature and some are not; some contain good things and some do not; some contain only sorts of things that we have thought of and some do not. It is plausible that there are infinitely many of these possibilities.

Our minimal possibility W^* is of course a possibility. But there is convincing reason to think that W^* is importantly unique. In the end, it does seem that reality could have lacked all contingent things. Given this, W^* includes only what must be, if there are any such things. Furthermore, what must be does not vary. There is no multiplicity of alternate realities, each of which includes only necessary things, but without containing all necessary things. If a thing is truly necessary, it is included in every last possible reality. Thus, W^* must have in it all necessary beings (if any), and only necessary beings. Also, no change is necessary. So any necessary beings in W^* do not change. They are just there.

If all of this is correct about W^*, then there must be just one minimal alternative reality. There is no way for two possible realities to contain the unchanging necessary beings, and nothing else. There would be no difference between 'them' at all, and so there would be just one possibility, not two. W^* is the unique minimal possible reality.

Thus, it seems clear that there are infinitely many possible realities with various contingencies, and only one possible reality without any contingencies. Each alternative reality is entirely possible. Each might have been the actual world. But now we are dividing the range of possibilities into those with at least one contingent thing and those with none. This yields infinitely many possibilities on one side and a single possibility on the other. From this perspective we can see that some contingency was *almost* bound to exist. The presence of some contingency was the closest thing to inevitable. If the one alternative reality without any contingency had been the actual world, that happenstance would have been a fluke of the most gigantic proportions.

Recall QM:

> *QM*: Why is there anything more to reality than the empty W?

The current statistical sort of response answers QM as well as it answers QC. If there are no necessary beings, then W^* is the empty W. So then W is the one and only alternative reality with no contingent thing. And again, something contingent was all but inevitable.

These observations do not quite completely explain why anything contingent exists. W^* remains a possibility. We have not seen a conclusive reason why the minimal possibility was not realized. What we may have seen is why it was *virtually* necessary that something more existed.

Conclusion

We have seen various candidate answers to our two main questions:

> *QM*: Why is there anything more to reality than the empty W?
>
> *QC*: Why is there anything that does not have to exist?

None of the answers is completely satisfactory. The statistical answer does not quite tell us why the maximally minimal possibility W^* did not turn out to be actual. Maybe this is as good an answer as we can get, though. We think that countless alternative realities could have been actualities, one of them being W^*. If so, then there cannot be an airtight reason why any one of them did not turn out to be the actual reality. They all had a chance.

FURTHER READING

Three essays that are worthwhile as further readings are 'On Explaining Existence' by Nicholas Rescher, 'Why is Reality as it is?' by Derek Parfit, and 'Why is there Something rather than Nothing?' by Robert Nozick. (The question addressed in Derek Parfit's paper is the question of why everything is as it is, which is different from our question of why anything exists, although it includes our question.) These essays are conveniently gathered together as the first section, 'Existence', of the following collection.

Steven D. Hales, *Metaphysics: Contemporary Readings* (Wadsworth, 1999).

CHAPTER 6

Free Will and Determinism

Theodore Sider

The Problem

Suppose you are kidnaped and forced to commit a series of terrible murders. The kidnaper makes you shoot a first victim by forcing your finger to squeeze the trigger of a gun, hypnotizes you into poisoning a second, and then throws you from an airplane, causing you to squash a third. Miraculously, you survive the fall from the airplane. You stagger from the scene, relieved that the ordeal is over. But then, to your amazement, you are apprehended by the police, who handcuff you and charge you with murder. The parents of the victims scream obscenities at you as you are led away in disgrace.

Are the police and parents fair to blame you for the killings? Obviously not, for you have an unassailable excuse: you did not act of your own **free will**. You couldn't help what you did; you could not have done otherwise. And only those who act freely are morally responsible.

We all believe that we have free will. How could we not? Renouncing freedom would mean no longer planning for the future, for why make plans if you are not free to change what will happen? It would mean renouncing morality, for only those who act freely deserve blame or punishment. Without freedom, we march along pre-determined paths, unable to control our destinies. Such a life is not worth living.

Yet freedom seems to conflict with a certain apparent fact. Incredibly, this fact is no secret; most people are fully aware of it. We uncritically accept free will only because we fail to put two and two together. The problem of free will is a time bomb hidden within our most deeply held beliefs.

Here is the fact: *every event has a cause*. This fact is known as **determinism.**

We all believe in causes. If scientists discovered debris in the upper stratosphere spelling out 'Ozzy Osbourne!', they would immediately go to work to discover the cause. Was the debris put there by a renegade division of NASA comprised of heavy-metal fans? Was it a science project from a school for adolescent geniuses? If these things were ruled out as causes, the scientists would start to consider stranger hypotheses. Perhaps aliens from another planet are playing a joke on us. Perhaps the debris is left over from a collision between comets, and the resemblance to the name of the heavy-metal singer is purely coincidental. Perhaps different bits of the debris each have different kinds of causes. Any of these hypotheses might be entertained. But the one thing the scientists would *not* contemplate is that there simply is no cause whatsoever. Causes can be hard to discover, or coincidental, or have many different parts, but they are always there.

It's not that uncaused events are utterly inconceivable. We can imagine what it would be like for an uncaused event to occur. For that matter, we can imagine what it would be like for all sorts of strange things to occur: pigs flying, monkeys making 10,000 feet tall statues from jello, and so on. But it is reasonable to believe that no such things *in fact* occur. Likewise, it is reasonable to believe that there are in fact no uncaused events—that is, it is reasonable to believe in determinism.

Our belief in determinism is reasonable because we have all seen science succeed, again and again, in its search for the underlying causes of things. Technological innovations owe their existence to science: skyscrapers, vaccination, rocket ships, the internet. Science seems to explain everything we observe: the changing of the seasons, the movement of the planets, the inner workings of plants and animals. Given this track record, we reasonably expect the march of scientific progress to continue; we expect that science will eventually discover the causes of everything.

The threat to freedom comes when we realize that this march will eventually overtake *us*. From the scientific point of view, human choices and behavior are just another part of the natural world. Like the seasons, planets, plants, and animals, our actions are studyable, predictable, explainable, controllable. It is hard to say when, if ever, scientists will learn enough about what makes humans tick in order to predict everything we do. But regardless of when the causes of human behavior are *discovered*, determinism assures us that these causes *exist*.

It is hard to accept that one's own choices are subject to causes. Suppose you become sleepy and are tempted to put down this book. The causes are trying to put you to sleep. But you resist them! You are strong and continue reading anyway. Have you thwarted the causes and refuted determinism? Of course not. Continuing to read has its own cause. Perhaps your love of metaphysics overcomes your drowsiness. Perhaps your parents taught you to be disciplined. Or perhaps you are just stubborn. No matter what the reason, there was some cause.

You may reply: 'But I felt no compulsion to read or not to read; I simply decided to do one or the other. I sensed no cause'. It is true that many thoughts, feelings, and decisions do not *feel* caused. But this does not really threaten determinism.

Sometimes the causes of our decisions aren't consciously detectable, but those causes still exist. Some causes of behavior are preconscious functions of the brain, as contemporary psychology teaches, or perhaps even subconscious desires, as Freud thought. Other causes of decisions may not even be mental. The brain is an incredibly complicated physical object, and might 'swerve' this way or that as a result of certain motions of its tiniest parts. Such purely physical causes cannot be detected merely by directing one's attention inward, no matter how long and hard and calmly one meditates. We can't expect to be able to detect all the causes of our decisions just by introspection.

So: determinism is true, even for human actions. But now, consider any allegedly free action. To illustrate how much is at stake here, let's consider an action that is horribly morally reprehensible: Hitler's invasion of Poland in 1939. We most certainly blame Hitler for this action. We thus consider him to have acted freely. But determinism seems to imply that Hitler was not free at all.

To see why, we must first investigate the concepts of **cause** and **effect**. A cause is an earlier event that *makes* a later effect happen. Given the laws of nature,[1] once the cause has occurred, the effect *must* occur. Lightning causes thunder: the laws of nature governing electricity and sound guarantee that, when lightning strikes, thunder will follow.

Determinism says that Hitler's invasion of Poland was caused by some earlier event. So far, there is little to threaten Hitler's freedom. The cause of the invasion might be something under Hitler's control, in which case the invasion would also be under his control. For instance, the cause might be a decision that Hitler made just before the invasion. If so, then it seems we can still blame Hitler for ordering the invasion.

[1] Chapter 9 discusses laws of nature.

But now consider this decision itself. It is just another event. So determinism implies that it too must have a cause. This new cause might be an even earlier decision Hitler made, or something his advisers told him, or something he ate, or, more likely, a combination of many factors. Whatever it is, call this cause of Hitler's decision to invade Poland 'c'. Notice that c also caused the invasion of Poland. For as we saw above, a cause is an earlier event that makes a later event happen. Once c occurred, Hitler's decision had to occur; and once that decision occurred, the invasion had to occur.

We can repeat this reasoning indefinitely. Determinism implies that c must have an earlier cause c_1, which in turn must have an earlier cause c_2, and so on. The resulting sequence of events stretches back in time:

$$\ldots c_2 \rightarrow c_1 \rightarrow c \rightarrow \text{the decision} \rightarrow \text{the invasion}$$

Each event in the sequence causes the invasion, since each event causes the event that occurs immediately after it, which then causes the next event occurring immediately after that one, and so on. The final few events in this sequence look like ones under Hitler's control. But the earlier ones do not, for as we move back in time, we eventually reach events before Hitler's birth.

This argument can be repeated for any human action, however momentous or trivial. Suppose an old man slips while crossing the street, and I laugh at him instead of helping him up. Using the above chain of reasoning, we can show that my laughter was caused by events before my birth.

Things now look very bad for freedom. Hitler no longer seems to have had a free choice about whether to invade Poland. I seem to have had no choice but to laugh at the old man. For these actions were all caused by things outside our control. But then what was morally wrong about what Hitler or I did? How can we blame Hitler for invading Poland if it was settled before his birth that he would do it? How can we blame me for laughing? How can we blame anyone for anything?

We can restate the challenge to freedom in terms of physics. Any action or decision involves the motion of sub-atomic particles in one's body and brain. These sub-atomic particles move according to the laws of physics. Physics lets us calculate the future positions of particles from information about (i) the previous states of the particles, and (ii) the forces acting on the particles. So, in principle, one could have examined the sub-atomic particles one hundred years before the invasion of Poland, calculated exactly how those particles would be moving one hundred years later, and thereby calculated that Hitler would invade Poland. Such calculations are far too difficult to ever complete in practice, but that doesn't matter. Whether or not anyone could have completed the calculations, *the particles were there*, before Hitler's birth, and the fact that they were there, and arranged in the way that they were, made it *inevitable* that Hitler would invade Poland. Once again, we have found a cause for Hitler's invasion that already existed before Hitler was born. And the existence of such a cause seems to imply that Hitler's invasion of Poland was not a free action.

And yet, it *must* have been free, for how else can we *blame* him for this despicable act? The time bomb has exploded. Two of our most deeply held beliefs, our belief in science and our belief in freedom and morality, seem to contradict each other. We must resolve this conflict.

Hard Determinism

The simplest strategy for resolution is to reject one of the beliefs that produce the conflict. One could reject free will, or one could reject determinism.

The rejection of free will in the face of determinism is called **hard determinism**. Think of the hard determinist as a hard-nosed intellectual who tolerates no softies. Free will conflicts with science, so free will has got to go. Here is a typical hard determinist speech:

> We must get used to the idea that no one is really responsible for anything. Belief in freedom and moral responsibility was a luxury of a pre-scientific age. Now that we have grown up, we must put aside childish ways and face the facts. Science has disproved the existence of freedom and morality.

Can we live with this depressing philosophy? Philosophers must seek the truth, however difficult it may be to accept. Maybe hard determinism is one of those difficult truths. Hard determinists might attempt 'damage control', arguing that life without freedom is not as bad as one might think. Society might still punish criminals, for instance. Hard determinists must deny that criminals *deserve* punishment, since the crimes were not committed freely. But they can say that there is still a use for punishment: punishing criminals keeps them off the streets and discourages future crimes. Still, accepting hard determinism is nearly unthinkable. Nor is it clear that one *could* stop believing in free will, even if one wanted to. If you find someone who claims to believe hard determinism, here's a little experiment to try. Punch him in the face, really hard. Then try to convince him not to blame you. After all, according to him, you had no choice but to punch him! I predict you will find it very difficult to convince him to practice what he preaches.

Hard determinism is a position of last resort. Let's see what the other options look like.

Libertarianism

If the hard determinist is the intellectually hard-nosed devotee of science, the **libertarian**[2] has the opposite mindset. Libertarians

---

[2] The use of the word 'libertarian' in politics is unrelated.

resolve the conflict between free will and determinism by rejecting determinism. Their guiding thought is that *people are special*. The march of science, subjugating observed phenomena to exceptionless law, is limited to the non-human realm. For libertarians, science is good as far as it goes, but it will never succeed in completely predicting human behavior. Humans, and humans alone, transcend the laws of nature: they are free.

What makes people so special? Some libertarians answer that we have souls, nonphysical sources of consciousness and choice that are not controlled by laws of nature. Others say that humans are indeed purely physical systems, but that they are not subject to the natural laws that govern other physical systems. Either way, laws of nature do not wholly determine human behavior.

Although libertarians are clear on what freedom *isn't*—namely, determinism—they have a little more trouble telling us what freedom *is*. They do not want to say that freedom is merely uncaused action. Saying *that* would equate freedom with *randomness*, and libertarians don't want to do that. Here's why.

Suppose Mother Teresa discovers a hand-grenade in an orphanage in Calcutta. As you might expect, she picks up the hand-grenade in order to dispose of it safely. But now an utterly uncaused event occurs: to her horror, her hand suddenly pulls out the pin and throws the grenade into the heart of the orphanage. The grenade explodes, resulting in mayhem and destruction. When I say 'uncaused', I really mean that there is *no* cause, none whatsoever. As I am imagining the example, the action of pulling the pin and throwing the grenade was not caused by any decision on Mother Teresa's part; nor did it have an external physical cause. No dormant dark side of Mother Teresa's personality has finally come to light. She has no nervous tic. Her hand simply flew up from absolutely no cause whatsoever. This clearly is *not* a free action. We could not blame Mother Teresa; she is the victim of a cruel accident.

The alarming thing for libertarians is that Mother Teresa seems *un*free precisely because her action was uncaused. Freedom now appears to *require* causation. This obviously threatens the fundamental libertarian claim that the key to the problem of freedom is indeterminism of human action. Libertarians must somehow distinguish between free undetermined action and randomness.

Some libertarians address this problem by postulating a special kind of causation that only humans wield, called **agent causation**. Ordinary mechanistic causation, the kind studied in physics and the other hard sciences, obeys laws. Mechanistic causes are repeatable and predictable: if you repeat the same cause again and again, the very same effect is guaranteed to occur each time. Agent causation, on the other hand, does not obey laws. There is no saying which way a free human being will exercise her agent causation. The very same person in exactly similar circumstances might agent-cause different things. According to the theory of agent causation, you act freely when (i) your action is not caused in the ordinary, mechanistic way, but (ii) your action *is* caused by you—by agent causation. If you freely decide to eat Wheaties one morning rather than your usual helping of Apple Jacks, it would have been impossible to predict beforehand which cereal you would choose. Nevertheless, your choice was not a random occurrence, for you yourself caused it. You caused it by agent causation.

It is unclear whether agent causation really solves the problem of randomness. Consider what an agent-causation theorist would say about your freely making a difficult decision. There are two important factors in decision-making: what you desire, and what you believe is the best means to achieve that desire. If you are undecided whether to vote Democratic or Republican, for instance, this is because some of your beliefs and desires favor a Democratic vote, and others favor a Republican vote. Suppose that, in the end, the set favoring a Democratic vote wins out.

A libertarian would say that mechanistic causes that occurred in the past did not determine this outcome. It was you yourself, via agent causation, that selected the Democratic vote. Your selection was subject to no laws; it was unpredictable. This activity of agent causation was not caused by your beliefs and desires. But now—and here is the problem—since the selection was not causally based in your beliefs and desires, it seems entirely *detached* from you. The selection did not emerge from what you know about the candidates and what sort of leader you want for your country. Your vote didn't arise from who you are. It just appeared in the world, as if by magic. Given this, it would be odd to praise or blame you for it. And this suggests that it was unfree.

Whether or not libertarianism relies on agent causation, its most worrisome feature is its clash with science. First, libertarians must reject the possibility of an all-encompassing psychology. Human behavior would be governed by the laws of such a science, and libertarians deny that human behavior is controlled by any laws. But the clash does not end there. Libertarians must also reject the possibility of an all-encompassing *physics*. The realms of psychology and physics cannot be neatly separated, for human bodies are physical objects, made up of subatomic particles. An all-encompassing physics could predict the future motions of *all* particles—even those in human bodies—based on the earlier states of particles. Since libertarians say that human behavior cannot be scientifically predicted, they must deny the possibility of such a physics. According to libertarians, if physicists turned their measuring instruments on the subatomic particles composing a free person, formerly observed patterns would break down.

This attitude toward science seems rash. Here in the twenty-first century, we have the benefit of hindsight on various disagreements between science, on the one hand, and religion and philosophy, on the other. Remember the Catholic Church's decision to censor Copernicus and Galileo for saying that the Earth moves around the Sun. No one wants to repeat that mistake. And remember the dramatic successes of science, both theoretical and technological. Of course, science is not infallible. But a philosopher had better have *very* good reasons to declare that an existing science is just plain wrong, or that a certain kind of scientific progress will never happen. One's philosophy should avoid colliding with or limiting science.

Our choices look grim. On the one hand, there is the dismal philosophy of hard determinism, which robs life of all that is distinctly human and worthwhile. On the other hand, there is the radically anti-scientific philosophy of libertarianism—which, given the problem of randomness, may not even succeed in salvaging free will.

Interlude: Quantum Mechanics

Before moving on, we should investigate a side issue—whether **quantum mechanics** bears on the problem of freedom. Quantum mechanics is a theory about the behavior of tiny particles. This theory was developed in the early part of the twentieth century and continues to be accepted by physicists today. Quantum mechanics (or at least, a certain version of it) is a radically indeterministic theory. It does not predict with certainty what will occur; it only gives *probabilities* of outcomes. No matter how much information you have about a particle, you cannot predict with certainty where it will be later. All you can say is how likely it is that the particle will be found in various locations. And this is not a mere limitation on human knowledge. The particle's future position is simply not determined by the past, regardless of how much we know about it. Only the probabilities are determined.

In the previous sections I was ignoring quantum mechanics. For instance, I assumed that if a cause occurs, its effect *must* occur, even though quantum mechanics says that causes merely make their effects probable. Why did I ignore quantum mechanics? Because randomness is not freedom. Let us try a little thought experiment. First pretend that quantum mechanics is incorrect and physics is truly deterministic. The threat to human freedom that this presents is what we have been talking about so far in this chapter. Next, in each person's brain, add a little lottery, which every so often randomly causes the person to swerve one way rather than another. This is like what quantum mechanics says really happens: there is an element of randomness to what events occur. Does the threat to freedom go away? Clearly not. If the original, wholly determined person had no free will, then the new, randomized person has no free will either; the lottery injects only randomness, not freedom or responsibility. And as we learned from the case of Mother Teresa, randomness does not mean freedom. If anything, randomness undermines freedom.

A libertarian might concede that quantum randomness is not *sufficient* for freedom, but nevertheless claim that quantum randomness *makes room for* freedom, because it makes room for agent causation. Imagine that it is 1939, and Hitler has not yet decided to invade Poland. He is trying to decide what to do among the following three options:

Invade Poland

Invade France

Stop being such an evil guy and become a ballet dancer

Quantum mechanics assigns probabilities to each of these possible decisions; it does not say which one Hitler will choose. Suppose, for the sake of argument, that the probabilities are as follows:

95.0%　Invade Poland

4.9%　Invade France

0.1%　Become a ballet dancer

After assigning these probabilities, the work of quantum mechanics is complete. According to some libertarians, agent causation now steps in. After quantum mechanics sets the probabilities, Hitler himself chooses, by agent causation, which decision he will in fact make. Physics sets probabilities, but *people*, by agent causation, ultimately decide what occurs.

If this picture were correct, then my criticism of libertarianism as being anti-scientific would be rebutted: agent causation could peacefully coexist with quantum mechanics. In fact, though, the coexistence picture makes agent causation a slave to quantum-mechanical probabilities.

Imagine running the following interesting (if wildly unethical) experiment. First produce one million exact clones of Hitler as he was in 1939. Then, in one million separate laboratories, reproduce the exact conditions that Hitler faced before he decided to invade Poland. Put each clone in his own laboratory and deceive him into thinking that it is really 1939 and that he is in charge of Germany. Then sit back and watch. Record how many clones attempt to invade Poland, how many attempt to invade France, and how many attempt to become ballet dancers. The coexistence picture says that you will observe a distribution of behaviors that roughly matches the probabilities listed above, for the coexistence picture says that quantum mechanics correctly gives the probabilities of outcomes. Thus, you will observe around 950,000 clones trying to invade Poland, around 49,000 trying to invade France, and around 1,000 practicing ballet. If you repeat the procedure again and again, you will continue to observe outcomes in approximately the same ratios. (The more times you repeat the experiment, the closer the total ratios will match the probabilities, just as the more times one flips a coin, the closer the ratio of heads to flips approaches one-half.) If you change the laboratory conditions faced by the clones, so that quantum mechanics predicts different probabilities, you will observe a new distribution of behaviors that fits the new probabilities. The distribution keeps following what quantum mechanics says.

What good then is agent causation? It seems to mindlessly follow the probabilities, having no effect of its own on the distribution of outcomes. This sort of agent causation is empty; it adds nothing to freedom or responsibility. Agent causation, if it is to be worth anything, must be capable of disrupting the probabilities given by quantum mechanics. There can be no peaceful coexistence: agent causation theorists must clash with science. Quantum mechanics does not help the agent-causation theorist. So I will go back to ignoring quantum mechanics.

We are back to the grim dilemma. Apparently, we must reject science or reject freedom. Yet neither option seems at all appealing.

Soft Determinism

Many philosophers believe that there is a way out of this dilemma. Others think that this way out is a big mistake. You must decide for yourself.

The way out is called **soft determinism**. According to soft determinists, our discussion took a wrong turn all the way back when we said that the available options were rejecting freedom or rejecting determinism. Soft determinists say that this overlooks a third option. We can have our cake and eat it too: we can retain *both* freedom and determinism. That way we can preserve both our science and our humanity. The argument in the first section, which concluded that freedom and determinism are opposed to each other, was a mistake. The alleged conflict is an illusion, based on a misunderstanding of the concept of free will. Our actions (or at least their probabilities) are indeed caused by events before our births. But they are often free despite this.

To explain what soft determinists are up to, let's first consider some examples. Imagine a very young boy with a serious misunderstanding of the concept of a *man*. This boy thinks it is part of the definition of the word 'man' that men never cry. As far as he knows, the men in his family never cry, the men on television never cry, and so on. He believes that his father is a man, of course, but one day he sees his father crying. The boy becomes very confused. Two of his beliefs now conflict: his belief that his father is a man and his belief that his father is crying. Which should he give up? Should he decide that his father is not a man after all? Or should he decide that his father was not really crying—that he was only cutting up onions, say? Obviously, he should do neither. Instead, he should clear up his conceptual confusion about the nature of manhood. Then he will see that his beliefs about his father's manhood and about his father's crying are compatible after all.

Here is a second example. How would you define the word 'contact', as in 'Barry Bonds's bat made contact with the baseball'? If you are like most people, your first answer is probably something like this: *things are in 'contact' when there is no empty space between them.* But now remember your high-school science. Baseballs and bats are made up of atoms. These atoms consist of nuclei and surrounding clouds of electrons. When one atom approaches another, the electrons of the atoms repel one another with electromagnetic forces. The closer together the atoms get, the stronger the forces become. Eventually the forces become so strong that they push the atoms away from each other. This occurs when the atoms get very close to each other, but before their clouds of electrons start to overlap. Thus, as Bonds's bat closed in on the baseball, the outermost atoms of the bat began to repel the outermost atoms of the ball, until eventually the ball came to a halt and flew in the opposite direction. At every moment there was some space between the bat and the ball. In fact, there is *never* absolutely zero space between bats and balls, nor between fists and jaws, fingers and computer keyboards, or any other things we consider to be in contact. Yet we all believe that contact regularly occurs. So we have another apparent conflict, this time between our belief in high-school science and our belief that things are regularly in contact. Should we renounce one of these beliefs? Obviously not. We should instead reject the proposed definition of 'contact'. Those who accept that definition are in a sense conceptually confused. For things can be in contact even when there is a small amount of space in between them. (What then is the correct definition of contact? Tough question! What about: *things are in contact when there is no visible space in between*? This is only a start.)

The soft determinist makes a similar claim about free will. Determinism seems to conflict with freedom only because we misunderstand the concept of freedom. If 'free' meant 'un-caused', then the conflict would be real. But that's not what 'free' means. (Remember Mother Teresa.) Once we clear up our conceptual confusion, the conflict will vanish. Then we can believe in *both* free will and determinism. Properly understood, they were never really opposed.

So far so good. But if 'free' doesn't mean 'uncaused', what *does* it mean? The soft determinist wants to say, roughly, that *a free action is one that is caused in the right way.* When you were kidnaped and forced to commit murders, your actions were unfree because they were caused in the *wrong* way. Free actions, such as Hitler's invasion of Poland, my writing of this chapter, and your reading it, also have causes, but they are caused in the *right* way. All actions have causes, but having a cause doesn't settle whether an action is free. Whether it is free is settled by what kind of cause it has. If free actions are those that are caused in the right way, as this definition says, then an action can be *both* free *and* caused. Thus, given this definition, freedom and determinism do not conflict.

Hard determinists and libertarians may object that all causes should be treated alike. So long as my choice is caused by events before my birth, it is unfree; it does not matter *how* it is caused. But for some purposes, soft determinists can reply, it is clear that causes are not all alike. Causing a running back to fall by tackling him is legal football; causing him to fall by shooting him with a crossbow is not. The rules of football treat some causes differently from others. According to soft determinists, we can think of freedom and morality in an analogous way. Morality, like football, has rules. These rules treat some causes differently from others. If an action is caused in a certain way—the right way—then the rules of morality count that action as free. But if an action is caused in the wrong way, then the rules count that action as unfree.

It is admittedly strange that my actions can be free even though they were caused by events that occurred before I was born. Some philosophers reject soft determinism on this basis. But given the implausibility of hard determinism and libertarianism, soft determinism at least deserves a fair hearing.

Soft determinists must refine their theory, though. When they say that free actions must be caused 'in the right way', what exactly does that mean? Examples were given: Hitler's invasion was caused in the right way; murders coerced by your kidnaper were caused in the wrong way. But examples are not good enough. We need a definition.

Here is a first stab: *a free action is one that is caused by the person's beliefs and desires*. This checks out with some of the examples. When kidnaped, your beliefs and desires did not cause you to shoot the first victim or to fall from the airplane onto the third. You did not want to do these things; your actions were caused by the beliefs and desires of your kidnaper. So the proposed definition correctly counts your behavior in those cases as *not* being free. It also correctly counts Hitler's invasion as being free, since the invasion was caused by Hitler's sinister beliefs and desires. Likewise, since my beliefs and desires caused me to write this chapter, and yours caused you to read it, these actions are also free, according to this definition.

But the definition's success does not last. Recall the second victim, whom you poisoned while you were hypnotized. If your kidnaper hypnotized you into *wanting* to poison the victim, then the poisoning *was* caused by your beliefs and desires. So the definition says that you were free. Yet you obviously were *not* free. So the definition is wrong. The soft determinist needs a better definition.

When you were hypnotized, you acquired beliefs and desires against your will. So maybe we should change the definition to say: *a free action is one that is caused by the person's beliefs and desires, provided that the person has freely chosen those beliefs and desires.* But this definition is **circular**: the word 'free' is used in its own definition. If circular definitions were kosher, we could have used a much simpler one: *a free action is one that is free.* But this is clearly unhelpful. Circular definitions are unacceptable.

(Circularity aside, it's not even clear that the modified definition is correct. I have freely decided to continue to work on this chapter. My decision was caused by my desire to complete this book. Is it *really* true that I have freely chosen this desire? I doubt it. I want to complete the book simply because that's the kind of guy I am. I didn't choose to have this desire; I just find myself having it. But this doesn't seem to undermine the fact that my decision to continue working is free.)

What about this then: *a free action is one that is caused by the person's beliefs and desires, provided that the person was not compelled by another person to have those beliefs and desires?* This new definition raises as many questions as it answers. What does the word 'compelled' mean here? (Philosophers always ask questions like this.) When you think about it, 'compelled' in its ordinary sense means something like: 'caused so as to destroy freedom'. But then it is circular to define 'free' in terms of 'compelled', for 'compelled' is itself defined in terms of 'free'. The circularity is not so blatant as when the word 'free' itself was used in the definition, but it is circularity all the same. So the soft determinist had better not be using 'compelled' in its ordinary sense.

The definition would not be circular if 'compelled' just meant 'caused'. But then the definition wouldn't work. Recall my free decision to continue to work on this chapter. The definition requires that this decision is caused by my beliefs and desires, and it is—by my desire to complete the book. The definition further requires that this desire is not caused by any other person. But one of the causes of this desire *does* involve other people: my parents instilled diligence and a love of learning in me. So if causal involvement by another person renders a desire compelled, then my desire to continue working is compelled. We all believe and desire as we do in part because of our causal interactions with others; no one is an island. So if 'compelled' meant 'caused', the definition would imply that no one ever does anything freely. That's not what the soft determinist intends.

Another problem with the definition is that not all compulsion is by another person. A kleptomaniac compulsively desires to steal, and so steals. But he is not free; he cannot help his compulsive desires. Yet the definition counts him as free. For his stealing is caused by his beliefs and desires, and he is not compelled *by another person* to have those beliefs and desires. We could just delete 'by another person'. The definition would then read: *a free action is one that is caused by the person's beliefs and desires, provided that the person was not compelled to have those beliefs and desires*. But the problem of the meaning of 'compelled' remains. It cannot mean 'caused' (given determinism, all beliefs and desires are caused). It cannot mean 'caused so as to not destroy freedom' (that would be circular).

Let's take one final crack at a definition: *a free action is one that is caused by the person's beliefs and desires, provided that those beliefs and desires flow from 'who the person is'*. The idea of 'who the person is' needs to be explained. Consider the case of hypnotism: after you snap out of your hypnotized state, you will be inclined to protest that poisoning the second victim did not result from 'who you are'. It was out of character for you. Even though you desired to poison him at the time (because of the hypnosis), that desire conflicts with the values by which you live at other times, and so did not flow from 'who you are'. The notion of 'who you are' can be further explained by distinguishing between **first-order desires**, which are desires to *do* certain things, and **second-order desires**, which are desires to have certain first-order desires. For example, you may have a first-order desire to spend every Saturday indoors playing video games, but a second-order desire to not have such an unhealthy first-order desire. If your first-order desires are caused by your second-order desires, then they flow from 'who you are'. But if you do not care at all about what you first-order desire, or if you do care but fail in your attempts to square first-order desires with your second-order desires, then your desires do not flow from 'who you are'. Thus, even though the kleptomaniac's thievery is caused by his beliefs and desires, it may not be free; for he may want very much to not desire to steal, yet nevertheless keep finding himself with this reprehensible desire. If his second-order desire *not to want to steal* has no impact on his first-order desire *to steal*, then this first-order desire does not flow from 'who he is'. And it is the first-order desire that is responsible for his pilfering ways.

This last definition may be on the right track, but there is still work to be done. First, the definition says that your desires under hypnosis do not flow from 'who you are' because they do not match the desires you usually have; they are uncharacteristic. But many perfectly ordinary free actions are caused by uncharacteristic desires. Though I am generally a nice person, a couple of times in my life I have irritably snapped at someone. Despite being uncharacteristic for me, my snapping was obviously a free action. So my desire to snap had better count as flowing from 'who I am'. Somehow, the definition must treat my desire to snap differently from your hypnotized desire to poison—even though each desire is out of character.

Second, compare two ways of *changing* 'who one is'. Way one: someone permanently brainwashes me into becoming a horrible person. The brainwashing is so thorough that for the rest of my life, I want nothing more than to harm people. At first, my actions seem out of character. But soon everyone forgets my former good qualities and regards me as a monster. Are my subsequent actions free? The question is hard, but it seems that they are at least partially unfree, since the new, evil 'who I am' results from brainwashing. Way two: I undergo *moral transformation*. After recognizing that my life is going badly and in need of reform, I change 'who I am', perhaps with the help of a spiritual leader, therapist, or other moral guide. (Moral transformation can also go from better to worse: we have all heard stories of promising young people who make the wrong decisions, fall in with the wrong crowd, and become self-destructive and immoral. The members of the 'wrong crowd' serve as negative moral 'guides'.) Unlike brainwashing, moral transformation does not destroy free will. But in each case, one acts in accordance with 'who one is', though that has changed under the influence of other people. Somehow, the definition must treat these cases differently.

Coming up with a good soft determinist definition of freedom is no piece of cake. Then again, who ever said it should be easy? Defining anything interesting is hard. (A few paragraphs ago, we couldn't even define a measly word like 'contact'.) And look at the alternatives to soft determinism: libertarianism ('I know from my armchair that physics is incomplete!') and hard determinism ('I reject everything good about humanity!'). If our first attempts to give a soft determinist definition of freedom don't succeed, we should just keep trying.

Gary Watson's anthology *Free Will* (Oxford University Press, 1982) contains a number of interesting papers on free will. See especially the papers by Roderick Chisholm, Peter van Inwagen, A. J. Ayer, and Harry Frankfurt. Chisholm defends libertarianism, van Inwagen gives a careful argument against soft determinism, Ayer defends a simple form of soft determinism, and Frankfurt defends a more sophisticated form of soft determinism using the distinction between first- and second-order desires.

Timothy O'Connor, *Persons and Causes* (Oxford University Press, 2000) contains an extended defense of libertarianism.

CHAPTER 7

Constitution

Theodore Sider

The Antinomy of Constitution

'It is impossible to hold just one material object—an ice cube, or a soda can, or a clay statue—in one's hand. Wherever there appears to be only a single material object, there are in fact two.'

Only a philosopher would dream of arguing for such a thing. As Bertrand Russell once said, 'the point of philosophy is to start with something so simple as not to seem worth stating, and to end with something so paradoxical that no one will believe it'. But mere shock value is not the aim. Philosophers grapple with arguments that have counter-intuitive conclusions because these arguments reveal hidden complexity in the world, even at the mundane level of ice cubes, soda cans, and statues.

Here is the argument for the counter-intuitive claim we began with. Ice cubes, soda cans, and clay statues are made up of matter. An ice cube is made up of water molecules, a soda can of aluminum, a clay statue of clay. So wherever there is a material object, there is also another object: a **quantity (piece) of matter**. Where there is an ice cube, there is also a quantity of water; where there is a soda can, there is a piece of aluminum; where there is a clay statue, there is a piece of clay. The ice cube, soda can, and statue are *made up of*, or **constituted** by, these quantities of matter. But they are not the same objects as the quantities of matter. For consider: the quantity of water making up the ice cube existed long before the ice cube was made. And if the ice cube is allowed to stand at room temperature, it will melt and so be destroyed, but the quantity of water will continue to exist. A sculptor begins with a piece of clay. By shaping it into the right form, she creates a statue, which did not exist beforehand. If she tires of the statue, she can squash it and so destroy it, though squashing it does not destroy the piece of clay. Thus, the piece of clay is not the same object as the statue, for it exists before the statue does and continues to exist after the statue is destroyed. Think of it this way. The sculptor began with a piece of clay. That's one object. She then created a new object, the statue. That's a second object. So after she finished sculpting, there existed two objects, the piece of clay and the statue. Thus, when I hold a statue in my hand, there are actually two objects there, a statue and a piece of clay. There only appears to be one, but there are really two.

The conclusion of this reasoning is that the statue and piece of clay are two different objects. But this is very hard to accept. Think of how similar to each other these objects are. For one thing, they are located in exactly the same place. Also, they are made up of exactly the same matter, which in turn means that they have exactly the same size, shape, weight, color, and texture. They are even more similar to each other than two duplicate billiard balls fresh from the factory, for such billiard balls are made up of different matter, and have different spatial locations. Given the similarity between the statue and the piece of clay, isn't it absurd to claim that they are two different objects? And yet they are; they must be, because the piece of clay existed before the statue, and could exist after the statue is destroyed.

This is an example of what the twentieth-century American philosopher W. V. O. Quine calls an **antinomy**: apparently sound reasoning leading to an apparently absurd conclusion. Philosophers prize antinomies, because they are bound to teach us something. Once caught in the antinomy, we cannot rest content with the status quo; something has to give. Either the apparently sound reasoning is not sound after all, or else the apparently absurd conclusion is not as absurd as it seems. Our job is to figure out which.

Assumptions of the Antinomy

To start, we must identify the crucial assumptions in the antinomy of constitution, especially any tacit assumptions we may be making without noticing. The most obvious assumption is:

> **Creation**: The sculptor really does create the statue—that is, the statue did not exist before the sculptor sculpted it.

The argument also makes some less obvious assumptions:

> **Survival**: The sculptor does not destroy the quantity of clay by forming it into a statue.
>
> **Existence**: There really are such objects as statues and pieces of clay.

And finally, the conclusion of the argument must really be absurd for the antinomy to bite:

> **Absurdity**: It is impossible for two different objects to share the same matter and spatial location at a single time.

Assuming there are no other assumptions we have missed, we must reject Creation, Survival, Existence, or Absurdity, in order to resolve the antinomy. Investigating these assumptions will shed light more generally on the nature of material objects.

The Just-Matter Theory

Let's begin with Creation, which says that the statue only began to exist when the sculptor shaped the piece of clay into statue form. Someone who wanted to deny this assumption could say instead that the sculptor creates nothing, but simply *changes* the piece of clay. Painting a red barn green creates nothing; it only changes the color of the barn. Likewise, it may be said, the sculptor merely changes the shape of the piece of clay from a rather lumpy shape into a statue shape.

This would avoid the absurd conclusion that two different material objects share the same matter. Just as the previously red barn is the same barn as the subsequently green barn, so the previously lumpy-shaped piece of clay is the same piece of clay as the subsequently statue-shaped piece of clay. When you hold the statue in your hand, you are holding just one thing: a piece of clay with a statue shape.

This response may be based on a general theory of the nature of material objects. Consider the **just-matter** theory, according to which hunks (quantities, pieces) of matter are the *only* objects that exist. A hunk of matter is defined by the matter making it up. The only way to create a hunk of matter is to create some new matter. Merely rearranging pre-existing matter creates no new hunks, it only changes old hunks. That is what happens when the sculptor shapes the piece of clay into statue form. Likewise, the only way to destroy a hunk of matter is to destroy some of its matter. Rearranging or even scattering the matter changes, but does not destroy, the hunk. So squashing the statue destroys nothing. The piece of clay has gone back to having a lumpy shape, but it still exists.

The just-matter theory leads to shocking conclusions—perhaps as shocking as the absurd conclusion of the antinomy that we're trying to avoid. We ordinarily think of sculptors as creating things. Likewise, we ordinarily think that freezing water in a freezer tray or shaping aluminum in a factory *creates* ice cubes and soda cans. The just-matter theory denies this. It says that the ice cube in your drink existed before it was frozen, though it would not then have been called an ice cube; your soda can existed long before it was shaped in the factory, though it would not then have been called a soda can.

A wrecked car is towed to a junkyard, where it is crunched, taken apart, and sold for scrap material. This destroys the car, right? Wrong, according to the just-matter theory! The quantity of matter we formerly called 'the car' has merely been scattered. All that metal (and plastic and rubber) still exists, sold to various people in different locations. Since none of the matter itself has been destroyed, the hunk of matter remains. The object we used to call 'the car' still exists, though we can no longer call it a car since it no longer has a car shape.

An even more extreme example: when Socrates died over two thousand years ago, his body was buried and then slowly rotted. By now, the matter that once composed him has been dispersed over the Earth's surface; some of it has even escaped the planet altogether. Still, none of that matter itself has perished. So according to the just-matter theory, Socrates still exists. Or, more accurately, the object we formerly called 'Socrates' still exists. We can no longer call it 'Socrates' or a 'person', since it no longer has a human form; it is now a scattered object, like a deck of cards strewn across a table. But it still exists. For similar reasons, the just-matter theory implies that you yourself existed thousands of years ago, for the piece of matter that is now you existed then. It was not then a person, since it was scattered across the Earth, but it existed nevertheless.

Maybe in the end we should accept these strange claims that the just-matter theory makes. But let's first look at some other options.

The Takeover Theory

We might instead reject Survival. In order to derive the absurd conclusion that the sculptor's work results in two different objects, we needed to assume that she created the statue (Creation), but we also needed to assume that she did not destroy the original piece of clay (Survival). For if creating the statue destroys the piece of clay, then at each point in the process there is only a single object, and we avoid the antinomy's conclusion.

Can a piece of clay *really* be destroyed simply by reshaping it? Though that's hard to believe, it shouldn't be dismissed out of hand. As we'll see, *every* response to the antinomy requires saying something a little strange. (That's what makes the antinomy of constitution such a good one.) We should instead ask for more information: *how* does reshaping the piece of clay destroy it? What general theory of objects justifies this claim?

The best answer is the **takeover theory**. An object, such as a piece of clay or a statue, is made up of certain particles of matter. Depending on how a group of particles are arranged, they will constitute an object of a certain **sort**, for instance, the sort *piece of clay* or the sort *statue*. When the clay particles in our antinomy were arranged in a lumpy way, they constituted a piece of clay. Later, after being moved around by the sculptor, they were arranged so as to constitute an object of a different sort, a statue. But according to the takeover theorist, particles can only constitute one object at a time. So as soon as the particles are arranged in statue form, the sort *statue* **takes over** from the sort *piece of clay*: the piece of clay stops existing, and in its place a new object, a statue, starts to exist. The particles no longer constitute the original piece of clay; that piece of clay no longer exists. The particles now constitute a different object, a statue.

An object's sort determines what kinds of changes the object can, and cannot, survive. Objects of the sort *statue* must retain a statue shape. So if the statue is squashed, and ceases to be statue-shaped, that statue stops existing; the sort *statue* hands control of the particles back to the sort *piece of clay*, and an object distinct from the statue comes into existence. At any one time, only one sort has control of the particles; at any one time, those particles make up just one object.

The takeover theory agrees with the just-matter theory that only one object can be constituted by a group of particles at a time. But the just-matter theory says that the sort of the constituted object, no matter how the particles are arranged, is always the sort *quantity of matter*, whereas the takeover theory says that the sort differs depending on how the particles are arranged. Appropriately arranged particles can constitute statues, ice cubes, or soda cans. This is certainly an advantage for the takeover theory: it means that not all objects are defined by their matter. Whether objects of sorts like *statue* and *person* persist through various changes does not depend merely on whether their matter continues to exist; how the matter is arranged is significant. Statues, for instance, go out of existence when they are squashed, even if their matter continues to exist. Neither are persons defined by their matter. Thus, Socrates no longer exists according to the takeover theory: when his body rotted, the sort *corpse* took over from the sort *person*, and the person that formerly existed—Socrates—ceased to be.

Still, on balance, the takeover theory seems worse than the just-matter theory. It says that the piece of clay is destroyed when the sort *statue* takes over from the sort *piece of clay*. Thus, one can destroy a piece of clay just by kneading it into a statue shape. Try convincing someone of *that* at your local bar! (Many would admit that a piece of clay can be 'transformed' into a statue, but the takeover theory denies a 'transformation', which is a way of continuing to exist, and insists on a replacement.) So *each* theory says something unintuitive about the changes objects can and cannot survive: the just-matter theory says that persons can exist after rotting and disintegration; the takeover theory says that pieces of clay *cannot* exist after acquiring more artistic shapes. So far the score is even, one strike against each theory. But now compare the theories in a more abstract way: which has a more intuitively satisfying *rule* for what objects exist? The just-matter theory has a clear rule: all objects are hunks of matter. The takeover theory provides no such clear rule. It does tell us what objects exist in some cases. It tells us, for example, that the sort *statue* takes over when the piece of clay is sculpted, and that the sort *person* relinquishes its hold when a person disintegrates. But what *general* rule tells us in *all* cases when one sort takes over from another?

Imagine a takeover theorist from Mars. Instead of sorts like *statue* and *piece of clay,* beloved of Earthly takeover theorists, Martian takeover theorists speak of sorts like:

outpiece: piece of clay located outdoors, no matter how shaped

inpiece: piece of clay located indoors, no matter how shaped

Earthly takeover theorists say that when a piece of clay is made into a statue, it stops existing and a statue takes its place. Of course, whether the clay is indoors or outdoors is irrelevant to what objects exist. Martian takeover theorists see things very differently. They view the world in terms of inpieces and outpieces, not statues and pieces of clay. When an outpiece is brought indoors, they say, the sort '*inpiece*' takes over, the outpiece goes out of existence, and a new inpiece comes into existence. This inpiece exists so long as the clay is indoors. Whether it is shaped into statue form is irrelevant to what object exists. But if it is taken outdoors, it stops existing and is replaced by an outpiece.

Earthly and Martian takeover theorists agree that the conclusion of the antinomy is absurd; they agree that there are never two distinct material objects made of the same parts. So each must think that the other is mistaken about what the correct sorts are, and about what objects exist. For consider the sculptor, inside her house, about to begin sculpting. The Earthling and the Martian agree that she holds a single object in her hand, but they disagree over what its sort is. The Earthling thinks that the object is a piece of clay, which will be destroyed when sculpted into a statue. The Martian thinks that it is an inpiece, which will survive being sculpted but will be destroyed when taken outdoors. They cannot both be right, since the same object cannot both continue and cease to exist. Thus, our own Earthly takeover theorist must say that the Martian is mistaken: inpieces and outpieces simply do not exist.

But how can this claim be justified? The Earthly takeover theorist's choice of sorts suspiciously mirrors the words we here on Earth happen to have coined. We could have invented different words; we could have gone the way of the Martians and introduced words for inpieces and outpieces rather than statues and pieces of clay. If we had, the Earthly takeover theorist must say, then we would have been mistaken in nearly all our judgments about when objects come into and go out of existence, for the true objects are pieces of clay and statues, not inpieces and outpieces. It is nothing short of a miraculous coincidence that reality just happens to contain objects matching *our* current words rather than those of the Martians. Believing in pieces of clay and statues to the exclusion of inpieces and outpieces would be anthropocentric.

Nihilism

Takeover and just-matter theorists agree that in any given case, there is a single sort of object present. The former's choice of *which* sort of object exists is suspiciously anthropocentric. The latter's choice is more objective, but has counter-intuitive consequences.

Since it is so hard to choose what sort of object exists in a given case, perhaps we should say that *no* sort of object exists. This is what the **nihilist** says. Thus, the nihilist challenges the assumption of Existence, according to which statues and pieces of clay are existing entities. If there simply are no such things as statues or pieces of clay (or inpieces or outpieces), then our antinomy does not get off the ground.

Is it wholly absurd to deny the existence of pieces of clay and statues? After all, we can just *see* pieces of clay and statues, can't we? Philosophers seek the *truth*; they are not merely trying to provoke, or annoy, or say whatever they can get away with. They often make surprising or unfamiliar claims, but these claims must always be reasonable; they should not directly contradict the evidence of our senses. Otherwise, even if we don't know exactly how to refute the philosopher, we may justifiably write him off as playing an idle game.

In fact, denying the existence of statues and pieces of clay isn't wholly absurd, and doesn't contradict the evidence of our senses. Consider the immense number of sub-atomic particles that make up what we call the statue. The nihilist agrees that these particles exist; she doesn't reject the existence of *everything*. Now, most of us think that, in addition to these septillion or so particles arranged in statue form, there also exists a septillion-and-first entity, namely the statue itself, which is composed of the septillion particles. But according to the nihilist, there is no statue. There are only the septillion particles, arranged in statue form; there is no septillion-and-first entity. In fact, according to the nihilist, the *only* things that exist are **particles**, that is, things with absolutely no smaller parts. Even protons and neutrons do not exist, for those things contain quarks as parts. Only the ultimate particles of physics (for instance, quarks and electrons) exist. The nihilist avoids the conclusion that the statue and the piece of clay are two things made up of the same matter by saying that neither the statue nor the piece of clay exists at all. Indeed, no objects larger than a particle exist—not even you yourself! There is no you; there are only particles arranged in person form.

Nihilism is not wholly absurd because everyday sensory experiences do not tell us whether there exist only particles, or whether there exist in addition objects composed of those particles. I (or rather, a number of particles arranged in 'me form') look in front of me and have a certain sensation, apparently of a computer screen. But that same sensation could be produced by mere particles arranged 'computerscreenwise'. How could I tell whether, in addition to the particles, there is also the computer screen? Even those of us who believe in computer screens agree that they look, feel, and smell as they do because of the arrangement of their septillion or so microscopic bits. So we must admit that the bits would look, feel, and smell the same regardless of whether they compose a septillion-and-first thing.

But even if nihilism isn't wholly absurd, and can't be disproven by simple observation, it is still pretty absurd. After all, following Rene Descartes, the seventeenth-century French philosopher, I can't disprove by simple observation that I'm not on Mars dreaming an extremely vivid dream. (Descartes himself thought that he could prove the existence of a benevolent God who would protect him from being so drastically mistaken, but his arguments are unconvincing.) I might pinch myself to see whether I am dreaming, but I could just be dreaming the pinch! Yet, philosopher though I am, I don't doubt for a moment that I'm currently located on the planet Earth. It seems reasonable to simply ignore the outlandish possibility that I'm dreaming on Mars. Now, it's hard to say exactly when it is reasonable to ignore such possibilities. But perhaps nihilism is outlandish enough to be in the same category as the dream scenario: difficult to refute but safe to ignore.

Anyway, nihilism may not even work on its own terms. It assumes that the world is ultimately made up of particles, that is, things with no smaller parts. But perhaps there are no such things as particles. Have you ever (late at night, perhaps in an altered state) entertained the hypothesis that our entire universe is just a tiny speck in a giant other universe? And that within each atom of our universe, there exists a whole other tiny universe? And that in each of the 'atoms' of this tiny universe, there is contained yet another universe? If this sequence continued forever, there would be no particles, since each object would contain smaller parts. I suppose these thoughts are as idle as Descartes's dream hypothesis, but a less psychedelic version is more worrisome: perhaps each particle contains smaller parts, if not an entire universe. When chemistry first discovered the atom, no one knew that atoms had smaller parts. Then protons, neutrons, and electrons were discovered. Still later, scientists learned that even protons and neutrons have smaller parts: quarks. As scientists develop more and more powerful tools, electron microscopes and whatnot, they keep telling us of smaller and smaller objects. Perhaps this process will continue without end; perhaps every object, no matter how small, has still smaller parts. In each of these scenarios, no particles exist, since every object has smaller parts. Now, *absolute nihilism*, which says that no objects at all exist, not even particles, is too silly to take seriously, for it cannot explain the evidence of our senses that objects at least appear to exist. So in either scenario, there must exist *some* objects; and given how the scenarios were described, these objects must have smaller parts. Nihilism would therefore be false in either scenario. Moreover, if some objects with smaller parts do exist, then there is no reason to deny that statues and pieces of clay are among these objects. And if so, we still face the antinomy of constitution. Nihilism does not help in the imagined scenarios, the second of which, at any rate, may for all we know be correct.

Cohabitation

Like the assumptions of Creation and Survival, the Existence assumption is hard to question. Since these are the only assumptions made by the argument, we are slowly being backed into a corner. The only remaining possibility is to question our intuition that the conclusion of the argument is absurd: in other words, to reject Absurdity. Perhaps two material objects can, after all, share the same matter and spatial location at the same time. We can call this the hypothesis of **Cohabitation**, for it says that the same region of space can be inhabited by more than one object.

Our problem has been to choose what sort of object sits in the sculptor's hand. The just-matter theorist says: a *piece of matter*. The takeover theorist says: a *statue*. The nihilist refuses to choose, and says: *neither*. The defender of Cohabitation also refuses to choose, and says: *both*.

Cohabitation seems strange, but are there any *reasons* against it? Yes; here are two. First, just before the sculptor squashes the statue-shaped clay, she allegedly holds in her hand two objects, a statue and a piece of clay. Then she presses her hands together, squashing the clay. According to the defender of Cohabitation, this destroys only one of the objects: the statue is destroyed while the piece of clay carries on. But the sculptor squashed the piece of clay just as hard as she squashed the statue; she exerted the same pressure with her hands on each object. So, we must conclude, the statue is far more vulnerable to squashing than the lump; it is much more delicate. But how can that be? The statue is *exactly like* the piece of clay in all of its physical characteristics. It is made up of exactly the same matter as the piece of clay, arranged in exactly the same configuration.

Second, the very idea that the same parts could make up *two* things clashes with the concept of a part. Here's an absurd story: 'A woman once decided her house needed a change, so she painted every part of it bright orange. But even though all its parts changed color, the house itself did not change color at all; it stayed exactly the same.' The story is absurd because it supposes that the house is something over and above its parts. Like any whole object, a house is in some sense nothing more than its parts taken together. But if this is right, then we must reject Cohabitation. If a whole is nothing more than its parts, then the same parts cannot form *two* wholes; otherwise one (or both) of the wholes would have to be different from its parts.

Four-Dimensionalism

We are running out of options! The argument for the antinomy made only three assumptions: Creation, Survival, and Existence, none of which is easy to deny. Defenders of the just-matter theory reject Creation, but are committed to the counter-intuitive claim that Socrates still exists. Takeover theorists reject Survival, but face the charge of anthropocentrism. Nihilists reject Existence, but are left with a theory too radical to believe. So the conclusion of the argument—that statues and pieces of clay are distinct objects made up of the same matter—follows. But accepting the conclusion, and therefore Cohabitation, itself faces two powerful arguments. What to do?

A remaining theory of material objects allows us to accept Cohabitation and to rebut the two arguments. That theory is **four-dimensionalism**.

Begin with the theory that 'time is like space', as discussed in Chapter 3. Think of time as a fourth dimension, alongside the three spatial dimensions. This is clearest in pictures. Consider the space-time diagram, Figure 4, that we saw in Chapter 3. The relevant feature of the diagram is that it depicts objects as having **temporal parts** as well as spatial parts, which is the core claim of four-dimensionalism. We tend to think only of spatial parts: a person's hands and feet, a car's doors and steering wheel. A person's spatial parts are spatially smaller than that person: they occupy smaller spatial regions than the entire person. But the four-dimensional perspective reveals temporal parts as well.

A person's temporal parts are temporally smaller than the person: they exist in a smaller temporal interval than the entire person. The diagram pictures a dinosaur, a person, and their temporal parts. Let's focus on the person:

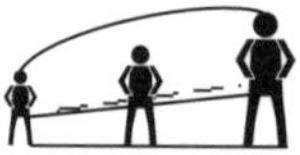

and her temporal parts:

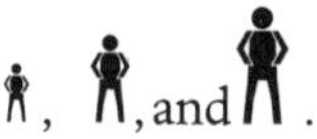

Each of these temporal parts exists at only one time, just as each of a person's smallest spatial parts exists at only one place. The person as a whole consists of all her parts put together, both temporal and spatial.

Consider the statue and piece of clay from the four-dimensional perspective (Figure 10). The diagram depicts a piece of clay which first has a lumpy shape, then is formed into a statue of a star, then is squashed back into a lumpy shape. The diagram depicts Cohabitation, since it depicts the statue as being a different object from the piece of clay. The piece of clay is the

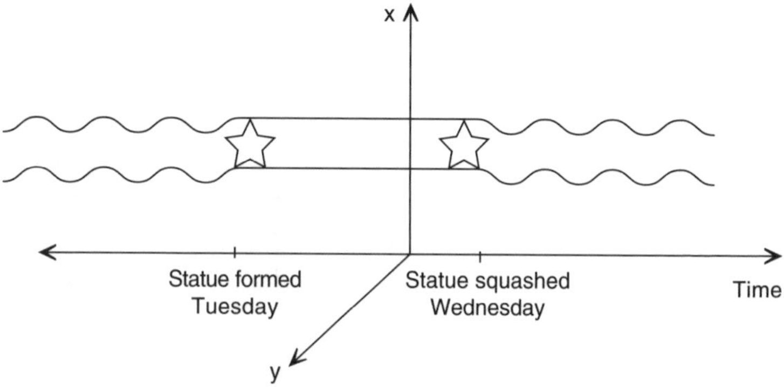

Fig. 10. Four-dimensional perspective on the clay statue

entire object, which begins long before being shaped into statue form and lasts long after being squashed:

The statue, on the other hand, is an object that exists only when the piece of clay is star-shaped:

As Figure 10 shows, the statue is part of the piece of clay. So the statue and the piece of clay are two different objects, just as you are a different object from your hand. Thus, four-dimensionalism embraces the conclusion of the antinomy, namely that the statue and piece of clay are two different objects.

We saw that Cohabitation faces two objections. Given the four-dimensional picture, the objections melt away. Let's take them in reverse.

The second objection was that Cohabitation violates the principle that a single set of parts cannot compose two different wholes. In fact, from the four-dimensional perspective, the principle is not violated at all. The space-time diagram clearly shows that the statue and the piece of clay do *not* have exactly the same parts. The piece of clay has more parts than the statue, since it has temporal parts located to the future of the statue:

as well as to the past of the statue

The statue and piece of clay only *appeared* to have the same parts because we were neglecting the fourth dimension of time.

The first objection asked how the statue can be so fragile when it is made of the same material as the sturdy piece of clay. To answer this objection, let us continue to press analogies between space and time. One useful spatial analog of the statue and the piece of clay is a long road and one of its smaller parts. US Route 1 runs up the east coast of the United States all the way from Florida to Maine; a short section in Philadelphia is called the Roosevelt Boulevard. The Roosevelt Boulevard is *part* of Route 1. They are of course two different roads, since Route 1 extends much longer (in space). But no one wonders why the Roosevelt Boulevard is so fragile as to stop existing at the city limits of Philadelphia, despite the fact that it is made of exactly the same asphalt within the city limits as is Route 1. Its termination at the city limits is merely the result of a decision by the good people of Philadelphia to use the words 'The Roosevelt Boulevard' for a mere part of Route 1. This analogy shows why the first argument against Cohabitation is misguided, given the four-dimensional picture. Why does only the statue go out of existence upon squashing? Answer: this is merely the result of our choice to use the word 'statue' only for the statue-shaped temporal parts of a piece of clay.

If you are still inclined to worry that the first objection threatens four-dimensionalism, this may be because of a mistaken picture of the two objects in the sculptor's hand, namely, a picture of two objects 'directly' present. If I touch your nose, I am in a sense touching two things, you and your nose. But your nose is the only thing I touch directly. I touch *you* indirectly, *by* touching your nose, which is part of you. The correct picture of the two objects in the sculptor's hand is analogous. There is just one object directly in the sculptor's hand, namely the current temporal part common to both the statue and the piece of clay.

The statue and the piece of clay themselves are in the sculptor's hand only indirectly, by containing a temporal part that is directly in the sculptor's hand.

If both the statue and the piece of clay were directly present in the sculptor's hand, then perhaps the survival or destruction of these entities would depend on their current physical characteristics, in which case we would indeed face the question of how the statue could be so fragile when the piece of clay is so robust. But since the only thing directly in the sculptor's hand is the current temporal part of both the statue and the piece of clay, what happens afterwards is just a function of the physical characteristics of the temporal part and what she does to it. If she squashes it, then there will be further temporal parts with lumpy shapes; if she leaves it alone, then those temporal parts will continue to be statue-shaped. There remains the question of what we will *call* various aggregates of temporal parts, depending on what those further temporal parts are like. We only call statue-shaped aggregates 'statues'. So if the sculptor squashes the statue and the further temporal parts have lumpy shapes, only the aggregate terminating at the squashing counts as a 'statue'.

Note that four-dimensionalism avoids the charge of anthropocentrism that the takeover theory faces. The English language contains a word ('statue') for collections of statue-shaped temporal parts of clay. It contains no words for collections of *indoor* or *outdoor* temporal parts of clay. Nevertheless, such collections exist. These objects are what the Martians would call 'inpieces' and 'outpieces'. Four-dimensionalism says that these strange collections are just as real as our familiar statues and pieces of clay. Compare the collection of segments of US Route 1 that are located within cities whose names begin with the letter 'A'. We have no word for this 'Route A', but it exists; it is just as real an object as Route 1. Thus, four-dimensionalists must admit the existence of inpieces and outpieces, *in addition to* statues and pieces of clay.

Some philosophers think inpieces and outpieces are strange entities, and dislike four-dimensionalism accordingly. Others dislike four-dimensionalism because they doubt that time is like space. Still others are suspicious of temporal parts: instantaneous objects popping into and out of existence at every moment. I myself have no problem with these things. Accepting inpieces and outpieces on an equal footing with statues and pieces of clay is an excellent way to avoid the charge of anthropocentrism leveled against the takeover theorist. Treating time like space has been fruitful in contemporary physics. As we have seen in this chapter, it is fruitful in metaphysics as well. Instantaneous objects popping into and out of existence? Perhaps that is a bit of a surprise. But any solution to the antinomy of constitution is bound to have some surprising feature. Otherwise the antinomy would not have vexed metaphysicians for so long.

FURTHER READING

The following article concerns antinomies and their importance in philosophy: W. V. O. Quine, 'The Ways of Paradox', in his book *The Ways of Paradox and Other Essays* (Random House, 1966).

Chapter 3 of Roderick Chisholm's book, *Person and Object* (Open Court, 1976) defends the just-matter theory (which is often called 'mereological essentialism').

Michael Burke defends the takeover theory (though he does not give the theory that name) in this fairly technical article: 'Preserving the Principle of One Object to a Place: A Novel Account of the Relations Among Objects, Sorts, Sortals, and Persistence Conditions', in Michael Rea (ed.), *Material Constitution* (Rowman & Littlefield, 1997).

Inpieces and outpieces are based on Eli Hirsch's 'incars' and 'outcars', introduced on p. 32 of his book *The Concept of Identity* (Oxford University Press, 1982). The primary question of Hirsch's book is: how do material objects continue to exist over time?

For further reading on nihilism, a good source is Trenton Merricks's book *Objects and Persons* (Oxford University Press, 2001), especially chapters 1 and 2. Merricks is not a true nihilist, since he believes in persons as well as particles. Close enough—he does not believe in statues or pieces of clay.

Chapter 1 of my book *Four-Dimensionalism* (Oxford University Press, 2001) is an accessible presentation of four-dimensionalism. Chapter 5 is a more technical discussion of the problem of constitution.

CHAPTER 8

Universals

Earl Conee

Introduction

Much of metaphysics is mind-expanding, especially **ontology**—
the part of metaphysics that is about the most basic kinds of
things. Philosophers engaged in ontology often argue that we
can find remarkable entities hidden in plain view. The entities
are supposed to be embedded in some familiar facts. They
are supposed to become apparent to us, once we think in the
right way. According to opponents of the entities, their apparent existence is an illusion. Whoever is right, we gain a better
understanding of the world by appreciating this sort of
dispute.

Think of three typical Red Delicious apples. It is a mundane
fact about them that they have several things in common. For
instance, they are red, they have grown on a tree, they are
composed of organic molecules, and they taste bad (that is the
sorry truth about Red Delicious apples, in spite of their self-
congratulatory name).

In line with some standard philosophical terminology, let's
use the term **property** for any feature of anything or anyone. Properties include color, shape, composition, location, temperature,

age, distance from the Washington Monument, ownership, mood, perceptual condition, educational status, marital status, and so on. A property is any way at all that something could be. We are assigning the term 'property' to those things, *if* they exist. So we are not sneaking in a controversial assumption here. Maybe there really are no such things as properties.

A bit more standard terminology: a property that can be a feature of more than one thing is called a **universal**. In other words, a universal is a way that numerous things could be—*if* universals exist.

We noted the mundane fact that three Red Delicious apples have features in common. This seems to be a fact that we can equally well state by saying that there are properties that the apples share. Properties that are shared are features of more than one thing, so they qualify as universals. Apples can't go around sharing universals that don't exist. These simple points seem to establish that universals exist.

The dispute over the existence of universals is one of the most durable debates in metaphysics. Can it really be that a few simple observations show conclusively that universals exist?

No. The question of whether or not universals really exist turns out to be highly challenging. Once we start thinking about them, universals are difficult to deny. The simple reasoning that we have just seen argues in favor of their existence, and there are other good reasons to accept them as well. If universals exist, then every object in the world has some. They are all over the place. Once they are pointed out, it can seem that no reasonable person could deny their existence. Yet the existence of universals turns out to be troubling and doubtful on several grounds. It can seem that universals would make problems and solve none. There are philosophical alternatives to accepting the existence of universals, but we shall see that the alternatives have troubles of their own.

Positive Reasons

Why not conclude that the existence of universals is proven by plain facts like the facts about shared features of apples that we have just considered? Would that be 'too easy'? What's wrong with easy? If the reasoning fails, exactly where does it go wrong?

We might try denying that the three apples have any properties in common. After all, strictly speaking, the apples do not have precisely the same color, and they differ in details of their chemical composition. Encouraged by these points, we might try to go all the way with this line and maintain that the apples have nothing truly in common.

This line is tough to defend. For one thing, it is difficult to get around the fact that one respect in which the apples are exactly alike is that they are apples. This seems to tell us that they have in common the property *being an apple*.

There is also serious science to contend with. Physics tells us that all electrons have exactly the same charge. So according to physics the electrons have this property in common. Charge is a property of electrons that plays a basic role in extremely well confirmed physical explanations of much of what happens in the world. It seems that we would have to argue against a basic claim of established science to deny that charge is a universal.

For another thing, suppose that we could finally defend the conclusion that no two things are exactly alike in any way. Still, the differences between the properties of things would appear accidental. For instance, even if the charges of all electrons turn out to differ minutely, that seems to be just a fluke. Regardless of the charge that any particular electron has, couldn't another electron at least happen to have exactly the same charge? Why not? What could absolutely guarantee that all charges are of different magnitudes? Nothing comes to mind. So the charge of any electron is a universal, since it is a sharable property, even if it is not actually shared. Although many things that are very similar in some way turn out to differ subtly, there are some ways that many things at least could have been. These are universals.

Here is another route to the existence of universals. Clearly, we see objects. But we also see the colors of some objects. Likewise, we see and feel the shapes and textures of some objects. The colors, shapes, and textures of objects are ways that those objects are, properties of the objects. Each of these properties is a way that other things are, or could have been. Since we see and feel the properties, they exist. They are sharable properties, and so they are universals.

Can this reasoning be reasonably resisted? We might try being skeptical about perception. Sometimes we make perceptual errors. We see something as having a feature that it does not have. Some philosophical skeptics about perception use such acknowledged facts of our perceptual fallibility to raise doubts that we ever *know* what perceptible features objects have.

The merits of such skepticism constitute a large issue in the area of philosophy that primarily deals with knowledge, **epistemology**. For present purposes, though, a defender of universals does not even have to dispute the skepticism. A strong perceptual argument remains for the existence of universals. Suppose that you see an apple as red. It can be granted that you do not thereby know that the apple is red, or even know that the apple exists. Nonetheless, it can be contended that the color red must be something. It is the color that you see the apple as having. So there must be such a color, even if this apple does not have it, and even if nothing has it. The mere fact that red is a way that you see an apple as being seems to imply that there exists such a way for things to be. Since multiple things at least could have been this color, it is a universal.

A further argument for universals deserves our attention, an argument about meaning. The argument focuses on what we are doing when we use language to formulate our thoughts. Consider simple sentences of the subject-predicate form, 'X is F', where 'X' stands for the subject (what the sentence is about) and 'F' stands for the predicate (what the sentence says about the subject). This is the structure of countless sentences, such as 'Alice is amused', 'Bob is baffled', and 'Carol is considerate'. When we use this sort of sentence to state something that we think, it is clear that the 'X' part, the subject, singles out our topic. What does the predicate 'F' contribute to saying what we mean? The natural answer is that we intend the 'F' part to say *how we take the subject to be*. In other words, we intend the predicate 'F' to express a property that we think X has, namely, the property *being F*. This intention is not often actively on our minds. But if we reflect, this intention is our best idea about what we are using the predicate for. When we think that Bob is baffled, *being baffled* is a way that we are thinking Bob is. So, there must be such a thing as this property. In these subject-predicate sentences, what we mean by the predicate is a property that many things can have. Therefore, what we mean by such a predicate is a universal.

Here is one last fast argument for universals. Red and blue are two different colors. So there exist two colors (at least). Any color is a sharable property. So universals exist.

We have seen reasons to think that an abundance of universals exist—colors and other perceived qualities, scientific magnitudes, and the meanings of unlimited numbers of predicates. Let's call a defender of the existence of all these universals a **universalist**. Why not agree with the universalists?

Doubts

We began with the fact that apples have things in common. But maybe this casually worded statement is misunderstood and inflated by the universalist. It sounds fishy to argue that apples or electrons have 'things' in common, and therefore these 'things', universals, exist. Just calling an apple 'an apple' does not seem like talking about two things: the apple and something else. Yet that is what the universalist argument implies we are doing. We are supposed to be saying something about both the apple and *being an apple*. That doesn't ring any bells. All we seem to be doing is classifying an apple as an apple.

The case for universals may not be in trouble here, though. Maybe we are talking about universals without realizing it. First, we should not confuse the claim that universals are **things** with the claim that universals are material objects. The universalist's claim is not that universals are entities of the very same type as protons, people, and pulsars—individual objects. Universalists just claim that universals are real, they are actual, and they are not merely apparent or illusory. They may exist and yet be different in nature from individual objects.

Also, in arguing that some true assertions about apples imply that universals exist, a universalist is not making a claim about what we actively think when we talk about apples. Perhaps we have a universal in mind only tacitly, as was suggested in the argument from meaning. The claim is that a universal has to exist for some of our factual assertions about apples to be true. This is supposed to follow because of what we actually assert, whatever we actively think that we are doing. When we classify apples as apples, for instance, universalists say that something could qualify to be classified as an apple only by exemplifying *being an apple*.

In any event, this point about seeming misinterpretation does not argue *against* universals. At most, it casts doubt on some lines of argument for universals.

The existence of universals does pose problems, however. Let's investigate the hypothesis that *being red* is a universal that is shared by the three Red Delicious apples. How does the universal relate to the apples? For one thing, where is it? There seem to be only two live possibilities for its location, and neither of them is attractive.

The first possibility is that universals do not exist in space. They exist, but nowhere. Things like apples that have universals are in space, but not the universals themselves.

This non-spatial alternative creates mysteries. How do we see the color of an apple, if the color is not there where the apple is? In fact, isn't it as obvious that we see the color located there, on the surface of the apple, as that we see the apple? More generally, if a universal is nowhere, then how does it get connected to some particular spatial objects and not others, in order to be had by some and not had by the others?

These may not be unanswerable questions. But the non-spatial possibility does not seem promising.

The other live possibility is that a universal is present wherever an instance of it exists. So *being red* is present where each of our three Red Delicious apples is, and where each other red thing is too. At least this puts the universal in the right place to be seen by looking at red things.

The whole universal *being red* cannot be just where one apple is, because other things are instances of the same universals. Is the universal scattered about in space, with part of it at the location of each red thing?

A scattered existence of parts would undercut the universalist theory. Universalists say that each of our three Red Delicious apples is red because they have one and the same thing in common, the universal *being red*. If each apple has at its location just its own part of the universal, then it seems to follow that what any one apple has is different from what any other one has. It seems to follow that they do not share the universal after all.

Suppose we try instead the idea that *being red* is located *in its entirety* where each red thing is. In this view, the apples definitely have something in common, the whole universal. The view seems to say something impossible, though. If the whole of the universal is where one apple is, how could that same universal be somewhere else too?

This turns out *not* to be blatantly impossible. We should distinguish 'wholly' from 'solely.' The claim we are now considering about the location of a universal is not the claim that the universal is *solely* in the spatial region occupied by that apple, and also elsewhere. That's blatantly impossible! The claim is rather that the whole thing is in a spatial region occupied by an apple, and the same whole thing is also simultaneously elsewhere. If it's wholly one place, then *all* of it is there. But this does not come right out and say that it is *only* there. So we do not contradict ourselves by adding that it is elsewhere too.

Multiple location is troubling, though. Universalists propose that the same whole thing—a universal—can be in more than one place at the same time. Well, if it can happen to universals, then why can't it happen to concrete things like *car parts* too? Imagine that some car is parked parallel to the curb with its right tires touching the curb. So, part of the car is definitely well within a foot of the curb. But maybe that part is multiply located. Maybe, say, the 13 inch wide portion of the car that is closest to the curb is somewhere else too. Maybe that whole portion is also on the other side of the car, doing double duty as both the left and the right 13 inch wide outer portion of the car. The rest of the car— the middle between the 13 inch wide outer portion—is definitely more than a foot away from the curb. So the *whole* car—all of its parts—is more than a foot away from the curb (although part of the car is *also* located within one foot of the curb). Now suppose that the law reads, 'It is prohibited for any whole parked car to be more than a foot from a curb.' With multiple whole location of car parts, you could earn a parking ticket no matter how carefully you parked! (If the law said instead, 'Part of the car must be within a foot of the curb', then that law would *not* be broken in our example. But it's more informative to think about the case where the law happens to read the other way.)

The multiple location of car parts seems silly. In the case of material things, we are strongly inclined to think that the spatial basis for distinguishing parts *has to work*. Suppose it does. We have no idea why it would work in some cases but not others. So maybe it has to work *across the board*. If that is true, then the universalist is mistaken in thinking that universals can be wholly located in many places at once. But then the universalist is in real trouble. The trouble is that, apart from multiple whole location, there seems to be nothing acceptable to say about the location of universals.

Another problem arises when we consider further the alleged role of universals in perception. Sometimes we see the color of a ripe Red Delicious apple. Suppose that this is seeing the universal *being red*. Does the universal itself have a color? There appears to be trouble for universals, no matter how this question is answered.

Suppose that the universal is colored red. Then it seems unproblematic that we see red when we see that universal. We see the color of the apple, and now we are saying that this color, the universal *being red*, is colored red.

On this alternative, though, there seem to be too many red things. There is a red apple and a red universal. We are supposed to be seeing the color of the apple. But now another red thing seems to get in the way, the color of the red universal. If that is what we see when we look at the apple, then it seems that we are not really seeing the apple's color after all, but rather we are seeing its color's color. And does *that* color have a color, or is it colorless? We are off on a wild goose chase. Something has gone wrong.

Suppose instead that *being red* is not itself colored red. We'd better assume that it is not green or yellow either, since any other color would equally get in the way of seeing the apple's color, and it would present us with the wrong color to boot. So we'd better assume that *being red* is colorless. On this alternative, when we see the color of the apple, we are seeing a colorless universal.

In familiar examples of seeing a colorless thing, such as seeing clean water, we don't see a color. So how come when what we are seeing is the colorless color of an apple, we see red? Again, something has gone wrong. Now we have trouble for both of the two possible alternatives concerning the color of universals.

Another doubt about universals arises in connection with relations. So far we have discussed only universal features, that is, ways that one thing can be on its own, such as *being happy* and *being an apple*. Universalists hold that there are also ways that things can relate to each other. They call ways of relating **relations**. Many relations seem to have multiple examples, just like features of single things. For instance, suppose that each of us has a brother. Yours is Bob and mine is Paul. Then it seems that there is a relation that you bear to Bob—the *brotherhood* relation—and I bear that same relation to Paul. If you and I are each carrying something, then we then both bear the *carrying* relation to something; if we are each the same age as some movie star or other, then we then both bear the *same-age-as* relation to someone, and so forth. These are examples where one relation seems to hold in many cases. According to universalists, these relations too are universals.

The new problem for universals concerns instantiation. To **instantiate** a property is simply to have that property. For example, when you are happy, universalists claim that you are instantiating the universal property, happiness. This claim seems to imply that there is a *relation* between you and happiness, namely, instantiation. Suppose that we apply the universal theory to instantiation, just as it is supposed to apply to other ways that things are related. Then your being happy includes you, happiness, and a third thing, instantiation, that relates you to happiness. This same relation of instantiation would likewise relate any other universal property to the things that have the property. So the universalist view implies that instantiation is a universal, a universal that is a relation. This seems to be what the theory has to say, and by itself, it does not seem bad.

But this is only the beginning. The theory now finds three things in the fact that you are happy: you, happiness, and instantiation. Yet if there are these three things in that fact, then they are related in a certain way. You are related to instantiation and happiness by bearing the instantiation relation to happiness. Concerning this claim, though, if it states a fact, then another application of the universalist view seems to imply that there is a fourth thing involved. The theory seems to imply that there is a 'bearing-to' relation that holds among the three things: you, happiness, and instantiation.

If there is any such fourth thing, then it does not stop there. Those four are also related, and so the theory says that there are five, and they are related, and so on without end.

We have witnessed an explosion of relations that do nothing but make connections between a thing and a property that it has. This seems way too complicated. When you are happy, your happiness is a condition that you are in; it is how you are. The connection seems immediate. Yet now we have a universalist theory telling us that there are endlessly many relations intervening between you and your happiness. It is difficult to believe in all of those relations, even for someone who considers universals sympathetically.

The extra relations are implied by the same explanatory principle that universalists use to infer the existence of ordinary relations. Universalists hold that related things are always related by some entity that is a relation. If that sort of principle has limits, what are they?

A universalist might say that instantiation is special. It is the maximally intimate relation that connects a thing to the thing's own properties. In this special case, the relation relates things directly without itself bearing any relation to the things that it relates. But however intimate a relation it is, how does it manage to relate those things without being related to them? And if instantiation can do that somehow, then why cannot things generally just be related, without any relation universals at all?

A Final Ground for Doubt

We are about to see that our reasons for thinking that there are universals seem to go overboard. For example, in the argument from meaning, a claim is made about a role that we intend for the predicates of subject-predicative sentences. The claim is that we think of a universal (at least tacitly) and we intend the predicate of a sentence to ascribe that universal to the sentence's subject. When we think that Alice is amused, we think of amusement in connection with Alice. For a wide variety of cases like this thought about Alice, the claim about attributing a universal when we apply a predicate seems harmless and maybe even correct. But there is a very powerful argument that requires us to deny that this is what we are *always* doing when we predicate. If the reasoning succeeds, it is a big problem for universalists. We'll see that it makes trouble for the main arguments for universals.

To appreciate this threatening line of reasoning, we can begin by noting the interesting fact that some properties seem to be instances of themselves. For example, all properties are, if nothing else, properties. If we apply a universalist view here, we infer that all properties share the universal, *being a property.* If absolutely *all* properties have this property, then so does that very property, *being a property.* It too exemplifies the universal, *being a property.* In other words, it is an instance of itself—a phenomenon that we can call **self-instantiating**.

Okay, that's interesting, at least a little. But it seems to be an isolated oddity. Most universals do not appear to be instances of themselves. To take a pretty much random example, we have no good reason to think that *being happy* is itself happy. In fact, that is out of the question. A universal is supposed to be a mere way of things. It does not have a mind capable of happiness. For another example, *being an apple* is no apple. When we count apples, we surely do not leave any apples out of our count by not including *being an apple* in the total!

It is easy to convince ourselves that universals are mostly like *being happy* and *being an apple* in that they are *not* self-instantiating. So we can formulate something that we believe as follows.

Being happy is not self-instantiating.

Now trouble arises. One assumption in the meaning argument for universals definitely goes wrong here. The meaning argument assumes that, in a sentence like this one about *being happy*, we use the predicate to attribute a universal to the subject. But in the case of predicating the denial of self-instantiation, it turns out that we *cannot* have in mind a universal that we intend the predicate to stand for. It would be the universal of *non-self-instantiation*. We cannot have in mind a universal of *non-self-instantiation*, because no such universal can exist.

To see why, suppose that a universal of *non-self-instantiation* did exist. Call this hypothetical universal 'UN'. If UN exists, then either UN does instantiate itself, or it does not. We will try each of these alternatives. It will turn out that both alternatives are impossible. That result reflects very badly on the existence of UN. Because UN implies the impossible, UN is itself impossible. UN cannot exist.

First, suppose that UN instantiates itself. Recall that UN is the universal that things have in virtue of which they do *not* instantiate themselves, if UN exists. So anything that instantiates UN, which we are now supposing includes UN, does *not* instantiate itself. This directly contradicts our current supposition that UN *does* instantiate itself. So our supposition must be mistaken. Since the supposition that UN *does* instantiate itself is a mistake, it clearly follows that UN does *not* instantiate itself.

So maybe that's the way it is. UN does not instantiate itself. What is the problem with that? Let's assume that UN does not instantiate itself and see what follows. We should again focus on what UN is supposed to be. UN is the universal that things have in virtue of which they do not instantiate themselves, if UN exists. Now we are assuming that UN exists *and does not instantiate itself*. So UN would be an *instance* of the universal that makes for things not instantiating themselves. Which universal is that? Well, if it exists, it is UN. So we have derived that UN *does* instantiate itself from the assumption that it does not. Since our current supposition that UN does not instantiate itself thus implies its own contradiction, this supposition too turns out to imply the impossible. So the supposition must not be true. In other words, it is not so that UN does not instantiate itself. Putting this more positively, we have derived that UN *does* instantiate itself.

We have just established that if UN exists, then it instantiates itself. Before that, we established that if UN exists, then it does not instantiate itself. Thus, if UN exists, an impossible contradictory situation is implied. No truth implies an impossibility. So we must conclude that UN does not exist. This might seem to be nothing more than a special problem for the peculiar candidate universal, UN. There's no such universal—but so what? Why is it worth the trouble of going through this fairly complicated reasoning?

The answer is that the reasoning undercuts the arguments for universals. We can argue for the existence of UN in the very same ways that universalists argue for the existence of any universal. These ways cannot succeed in establishing the existence of UN, since we've just seen that UN does not exist. So there must be something wrong with the arguments for universals. That is a big deal.

For instance, the reasoning about meaning begins with an apparent psychological fact about something that we intend each predicate to do for us. We are supposed to intend the predicate to stand for a universal. The argument infers that the intended universals exist. Now we see that in at least one case the intention cannot get us a universal. Since UN does not exist, there is no such thing for us to mean by the predicate 'does not instantiate itself'. If the reasoning about meaning definitely does not prove the existence of a universal in this case, why think that it *ever* works?

Our first argument for universals, the argument about apples having things in common, becomes similarly suspect. The something-in-common reasoning can be applied to properties as well as to apples. The properties of *being happy* and *being an apple* seem to have much in common. They are both properties, both are instantiated by many things, and so on. Crucially, each does not instantiate itself. From this, by the standard universalist inference, we would have it that *non-self-instantiation*, UN, is something that those properties share. Yet we have seen that UN does not exist. Since this sort of reasoning does not *always* work, why think that it *ever* does?

The argument from the apparent use of certain universals in science is not as conspicuously subject to the same problem. But in the end, the problem is there. Science does not appeal to UN to explain physical phenomena. But the argument from science infers, for instance, that charge is a universal. It gets this consequence from the fact that there are scientific explanations that assert the presence of the same charge in many things. Maybe the truth of such claims does not really require the existence of a universal. Maybe they manage to be true in whatever way the following claim succeeds in being true:

> One way in which *being an apple* is the same as *being happy* is that each does not instantiate itself.

This statement is unlikely to turn up in a normal conversation. But it is true. It is true somehow, without any help from UN.

So maybe the scientific claim that electrons have the same charge likewise manages to be true without any help from a universal.

Thus, the argument for the conclusion that UN does not exist turns out to be unnerving to a universalist. It makes all of the inferences to existence of universals look dubious. On further investigation, these doubts about the existence of universals may not hold up. The problems do make many philosophers doubtful of the universalist view.

Alternatives

What are the philosophical alternatives to accepting the existence of the abundance of universals accepted by the universalist?

Sparse Universals

The nearest alternative view is that there are universals, but not as many as the universalist accepts. There is not a different universal every time there is some apparent difference in the ways of things. Rather, universals are comparatively sparse. In particular, there are no negative universals, like *not being an apple* and *non-self-instantiation*. Perhaps there are also no universals that serve as meanings of ordinary predicates like 'happy' and 'red'. David Armstrong, a leading contemporary proponent of the sparse universals idea, holds that only properties used in scientific explanations are genuine universals.

This new approach has drawbacks. It might seem to have the advantage of avoiding the problem of UN in a principled way, by denying reality to all 'negative' universals. The notion of negativity is nebulous, though. For instance, the predicate 'unoccupied space' sounds very negative. But what about 'empty space'? That seems to mean the same thing, without being at all clearly negative. And what about 'pure space'? That seems to mean the same thing again, while sounding positively positive. Even *non-self-instantiation* itself might be characterized as the property of being 'only externally instantiated', which is not clearly negative. So if the view is described in part as a denial that 'negative' universals exist, then this part of the view is gravely obscure.

Another problem for a sparse approach to universals is that of finding a defensible principle to identify the genuine universals. Do the predicates of all self-proclaimed 'sciences' symbolize genuine universals? Including political science? Creation science? If not, what are the restrictions? Also, there is fully legitimate science that turns out to be mistaken. Do predicates in a mistaken scientific theory identify genuine universals? If so, then why is a mistaken theory a better guide to reality than a complete fiction? If not, then maybe no current scientific predicate identifies a universal, because we may not yet have any scientific theory that is entirely correct. Maybe no one will pursue science long enough and well enough to find the whole truth. If so, then there will never be an entirely true and complete science to rely on in order to specify the real universals. But then which are the sparse universals that actually exist, if not those used by the true and complete science?

The sparse approach does not solve the problem about the location of universals. No matter how few universals are instantiated, they pose the problematic alternatives of multiple location and lack of location. So that difficulty remains.

A final problem is that the sparser are the universals that a philosophical view invokes, the more difficult it is for the view to explain the things for which universals seem suited. For one example of principled austerity about universals, there is the elegant worldview that defers entirely to basic physics. It holds that all that is real is the minimum that is needed to explain the most basic physical states and changes in things. Concerning universals, the view is that only the basic predicates of the ultimate and true physics symbolize universals. This elegant sparse universal theory seems not to provide for some facts about genuine possibilities. For instance, it seems to be a fact that some other properties could have been the fundamental physical properties of things. For instance, physicists draw inferences about how the universe would have developed differently if various alternative properties had been the basic magnitudes. Suppose it is a fact that there are certain alternative properties that could have been physically fundamental. If so, then the sparse universalism that admits the existence of only the properties of the actual ultimate physics is incomplete. The properties that might have been fundamental are left out.

Tropes

One step farther away from the abundance of universals accepted by the universalist is the theory of 'tropes'. A trope is a property. It is a way that some one thing is. But a trope is a particular thing, not a universal. Each trope can be instantiated by *only* one entity. The red color of a particular fire hydrant is one trope; the color of any other hydrant is another trope, even if the hydrants are the very same shade of red. (In fact, strictly speaking, each red part of a hydrant has its own trope of redness.)

'Tropical theory', as we can call it, seems to avoid the location difficulty for universals. Since a trope has one instance, each trope can be wholly located in the one place where its instance is. Tropical theory is well equipped to agree with the argument that concluded that a universal of *non-self-instantiation* does not exist. Suppose that you are happy. Then one trope is your happiness—it is yours alone. Your happiness trope does have *a* property of *non-self-instantiation*. That property is a trope. Does this particular *non-self-instantiation* trope that is had by your happiness also have itself? No. Precisely because it is a trope, it has only one instance. And again, that instance is your happiness. So it definitely does not have any other instance, including itself.

(Since that trope of *non-self-instantiation* does not instantiate itself, it might have its own *different* trope of *non-self-instantiation*. So there may be an infinite sequence here, but at least there is no contradiction. That is an improvement.)

Tropical theories have troubles of their own, though. For instance, suppose that it is a fact that two fire hydrants just happen to be *identical* in shape. Why is that a fact, in spite of the non-identity of their shape tropes? Typically, a tropical theorist will say that the shape tropes of the two hydrants are correctly said to be 'identical' when those shape tropes *maximally resemble* one another. What we casually call 'identity' of shape is really just a maximal likeness of shapes.

The shapes we count as identical need not be maximally alike, however. Suppose that the two hydrants are exactly alike in shape, but they differ in size. The shape trope of the larger hydrant is spread out over a larger area than is the shape trope of the smaller hydrant. Suppose that a third hydrant matches the first one in both shape and size. If so, then the shape tropes of the first two hydrants are not *maximally* alike. They are not as much alike as are the shape tropes of the first and the third hydrants, which are alike in both shape and size. Yet this does not interfere at all with the fact that first two hydrants are identical in shape. Tropical theorists need another explanation of this sort of identity.

Sets

Theorists who take the next step away from abundant universals agree about the existence of lots of universals. They seek to identify universals with certain things that are familiar from other inquiries. The classic version of this view holds that each universal is identical to a *set* of things. The universal *being red*, for instance, is the set of things that are red.

Sets are familiar mathematical objects, useful for various theoretical purposes. A key fact about sets is that they are identical exactly when they have the same members. The membership of a set is the whole story about which set it is. Because of this, sets are often described by simply itemizing their members within curly brackets, for example, {Art, Bill} is the set whose members are Art and Bill, while {1,2,3, . . . } is the set of the positive integers. Sets are very well understood in some ways. It would be intellectually comforting if universals turned out to be sets.

The view that a universal is a set of instances diverges from abundant universalism in some cases. The abundant theory allows there to be different universals wherever there is any apparent difference in how things are. For example, 'phlogisticated air' was supposed to be air that is infused with the substance phlogiston, and this was supposed to help to explain combustion. It turns out that there is no such substance. So nothing really has the property *being phlogiston*. Salem, Massachusetts was supposed to have had resident witches who were dealing with the Devil. But it did not. Nothing really had the property *being a Devil-dealing Salem witch*. The properties, *being phlogiston* and *being a Devil-dealing Salem witch*, seem quite different from one another. The former would be exemplified by air and it would help to explain fire; the latter would be exemplified by people and it would imply engaging in supernatural transactions. The set view, though, does not allow for different universals here. A basic fact about sets is that there are two sets only when their memberships differ. The membership of the set of things that are phlogiston is exactly the same as the membership of the set of things that are Devil-dealing Salem witches. In each case, there are none. So in each case the set of instances is the set with no members, the null set. Yet in light of the apparent differences, how could there be just one universal here?

Another drawback of the set view concerns the composition of facts. Simple facts seem to be composed of the things that make them true. For instance, the fact that you are happy (assuming that it is a fact) definitely involves you. So it seems fine to include you in the constitution of that fact. The fact also involves happiness, if there is such a universal. So that universal seems to belong in the constitution of the fact, too. But the fact that you are happy seems not to involve Oprah Winfrey at all. (We can suppose that your happiness does not derive from Oprah in any way, just to keep her out of it altogether.) Yet Oprah is a happy person. So she is a member of the set of happy individuals. A set is somehow made up of its members. Thus, if happiness is identical to the set of happy individuals, then Oprah is in some way involved in the make up of happiness. She would be thereby involved in the fact that you are happy. That seems wrong.

Nominalism

The most drastic departure from abundant universalism goes all the way away. Classic nominalism holds that there are no properties at all, no universals of any sort, whether sets or not, and no tropes. There are only particular objects. We apply a *word* like 'red' to many things, but not because those things share a universal. Since nominalism dispenses with universals, it seems to have none of the troubles that we have been considering.

Nominalists have to be careful in order to succeed in doing without universals while appealing to words. The word 'red,' for example, seems to have many instances, both written and spoken. Each word thus appears to have the generality that is characteristic of universals. To cope with this, many nominalists restrict their theories to using only particular written marks and sounds instead of words. When I pronounce 'red' and you pronounce 'red', we say 'the same word' with these two sounds. Nominalists try to account for this sort of 'same-word' fact while denying that any universal is shared by the two sounds.

The main difficulty for nominalism is to explain the phenomena that give rise to arguments for the existence of universals. For instance, there is the basis for our last fast initial argument for universals. It relies on the nearly indisputable fact that blue is a color. This seems to be a fact about the property *being blue*. How can it be a fact, if there is no such thing as that property?

Nominalists have proposed paraphrases. They have claimed that sentences stating facts that appear to require the existence of properties really state no such facts. They have used other sentences to try to show this. These other sentences are supposed to say the same as the originals, while not even appearing to require universals.

In particular, 'Blue is a color' seems to be about the universal *being blue*. Its subject term, 'Blue', seems to refer to that property. A nominalist can claim that the same fact is also stated in this way: 'Each blue thing is a colored thing.' In this sentence, the word 'blue' does not appear to refer to an object, because it is not a noun. The word here is just an adjective.

Nominalists who say this have to be able to explain how these adjectives work while using nothing but particular objects. That is not easy. Why does the word 'blue' apply to the things that it does, and not apply to other things? A nominalist can say, 'The word "blue" applies as it does because English speakers chose "blue" as a term for blue things and consequently it applies to things that are indeed blue.'

This nominalist claim relies on our prior understanding of the word 'blue'. That is not cheating, though. We are not asking how to interpret the word. We are just asking why the word applies as it does, given how we understand it.

The answer seems to leave something out, however. It does not tell us what makes it true that those things are blue. This is not a *causal* question. Nominalists can offer common sense and science about what causes some things to become blue and what causes some things to stay blue. But as for explaining what a thing's being blue consists in, nominalists must say, 'The things that are blue just are blue, and that is the end of the story.'

Explanations all end somewhere, but it is difficult to be satisfied with this stopping place.

Nominalists can observe that we do not add an awful lot of explanatory oomph just by saying, 'What makes it true that an object is blue is that there is an entity, the universal *being blue*, and the object instantiates that entity.' For full understanding, we need to know more about the alleged universal and more about instantiation. And we have seen trouble in attempts to explain these things. Yet in spite of the troubles, invoking a universal does seem to be the start of an explanation of what something's being blue consists in. The nominalist refuses all further explanation here.

Whether or not the nominalist position about this is acceptable, the nominalist paraphrasing tactic to avoid commitment to the existence of universals while explaining the truth of sentences seemingly about universals sometimes fails. Other sentences seemingly about universals cannot be paraphrased in the same way as 'Blue is a color'.

Consider the sentence 'Sloth is a vice.' That is true. But it does not say the same thing as the paraphrase, 'Every slothful thing is a vicious thing.' The latter sentence is *not* true. Someone who has the relatively minor vice of sloth may be otherwise so virtuous that he or she is in no sense vicious.

A replacement for this paraphrase is available: 'Every slothful thing has at least one vice.' That matches the original sentence in that it is true too. Trouble for a nominalist arises from the noun 'vice' at the end. It appears that 'vice' refers to something that the sentence says is had by any slothful thing. Seemingly, this would be the property *being a vice*. Nominalists deny that any property exists. So they need a different paraphrase, or a different account of the truth of the sentence.

Nominalists also need some explanation of plausible claims that seem to be explicitly about properties. We illustrated a problem for sparse universalists with the claim: 'some other properties could have been the fundamental physical properties of things'. This claim appears to be a truth about properties. Nominalists must deny that. They may say that it is true, but not really about properties, or they may say that it is not really true at all. To defend either claim, they have explanatory work to do.

Conceptualism

The word 'apple' applies to many things—the apples. Why? Universalists say that the word applies to things that share the universal that we associate with 'apple', namely, *being an apple*. As we saw, universalism has trouble, including problems of location and instantiation. Nominalists agree that the word 'apple' applies to the apples, but they deny that anything common to the apples makes the word apply to them. As we saw, nominalism has trouble, including the difficulty in accounting for the application of an adjective without relying on an entity that gives the word its application. Maybe we can split the difference between the two approaches and come out all right.

Conceptualism is the view that the things that confer generality on our words are certain things in our minds, namely, concepts. A **concept** is a means by which we can think of things. We have the concept of a boat. Our concept of a boat applies to boats, and not anything else. The concept is general in that way. By adopting the word 'boat' to stand for this concept, we give the word the general application to boats that the concept has built into it. That is the account of conceptualism. The account gives conceptualists something with the desired generality—the concept—while allowing them to deny that any one entity is shared by all of the boats.

(An aside about philosophy and practical life: conceptualism can be thought of as a friendly compromise. Neither universalism nor nominalism is entirely vindicated, while each is borne out to some extent. That seems nice. But the compromising character of conceptualism is a neutral fact about it, not a strength. We don't need to make peace and move on. The metaphysical problem of universals is neither a war nor a game. The problem is a purely intellectual challenge. If conceptualism retains what is correct in universalism and in nominalism and conceptualism offers an adequate explanation of the phenomena under consideration, then it solves the problem. Some who accept other views might still reject it because it leaves out features of the other views that they cherish. Their rejection would not affect the merits of the solution. The philosophical aim is to know the truth of the matter, not to achieve reconciliation among disputants. On the other hand, if conceptualism does not solve the intellectual problem, then we can decline to accept it without being in any trouble. We can decline to accept all of the alternatives. We don't need a solution to this problem in order to go on with our lives. It is not a practical difficulty that must be solved in order to live well. We can keep thinking about it at our leisure.)

Back to the issue. Conceptualism confronts criticism. The simple argument for universals that got us started uses some mundane facts, such as the fact that three Red Delicious apples are alike in having grown on a tree. This seems to be a fact constituted entirely outside of our minds. It is constituted partly by the apples. Perhaps the rest of the constitution of the fact is a universal that the apples share, or perhaps it is a resemblance among some tropes that each apple instantiates, or perhaps it is something else. In any case, it seems that the rest of the fact is something that pertains to the apples and not to us. Conceptualists locate the apples out there, but not the rest of the fact. A mental thing, the concept of having grown on a tree, is supposed to be the rest of what explains the fact that the apples have in common having grown on a tree. Yet the mind seems to be the wrong place to locate any part of that fact.

Explaining how a concept gets its particular application is also problematic. We are familiar with one initially promising way to give some things a kind of multiple application, but it turns out not to help. We can give multiple application to a word by a procedure of pointing and stipulating. The procedure does not rely on any common element in the things to which it applies. For instance, we can start with a meaningless term, say, 'blurg.' We can stipulate that the things to which 'blurg' applies are those that we point at, and then point at this thing, that thing, and the other thing. Thereafter, the term 'blurg' applies to this, that, and the other, whether or not they have anything in common.

This procedure does not develop a *concept* of a blurg though. The term 'blurg' does not get associated with any *way of thinking* of the three things. We have simply labeled those things as 'blurg' without attaching any general meaning to the label. Also, even if some procedure like this could assign some concept an application, the concept thereby applies only to the things that we have singled out. Yet generally our concepts are not restricted in that way. For instance, there are constantly new and previously unknown things to which our concept of blue applies—they are new blue things. Clearly we did not single them out in setting up our concept of blue. So a 'blurg'-like specification of a concept's application would not explain why the concept of blue applies to the new things.

A conceptualist can say that we do not have to *do* anything to assign things to concepts. When we acquire concepts, they are already equipped with applications. Concepts have their applications intrinsically. They just do apply to certain things—that is their nature.

An account of concept application that stops there is problematic. It compares unfavorably to the nominalist explanation of why general words apply as they do, and we were none too happy about that one. The nominalist says that the word that we intend for blue things, 'blue', applies to those things because they are blue and that's that. However incomplete this account may be, it must be at least part of the truth that 'blue' applies to things because they are blue. In contrast, the conceptualism that we are now considering holds that the concept of blue applies where it does *because it just does*. This is not virtue of anything we do to relate the concept to blue things and it is not in virtue of anything about the blue things themselves. End of story. That answer indicates no basis in the blue things for the application of the concept. Yet something about blue things surely seems to be part of why they are truly called 'blue'.

These are not conclusive objections to conceptualism. They do make for troubling explanatory challenges to the view.

Conclusion

We have seen problems for many approaches to the question of whether universals exist. There is more philosophy about this, but it doesn't get any easier. The problem of universals is a tough one. A consolation is that it is intellectually enriching to appreciate the strengths and weaknesses of the alternative approaches.

FURTHER READING

D. H. Mellor and Alex Oliver (eds.), *Properties* (Oxford University Press, 1997) is a collection of recent essays about universals by defenders of several approaches. The introductory chapter very helpfully describes the included essays.

Alex Oliver, 'The Metaphysics of Universals', *Mind*, 105 (1996), 1–80, is a critical survey of recent philosophical work on universals. It includes an extensive bibliography.

CHAPTER 9

Possibility and Necessity
Theodore Sider

The Problem of Possibility and Necessity

Given a team of scientists, unlimited time and resources, and enough patience, you could observe a lot about the world. You could observe the behavior of electrons, protons, atoms, molecules, organisms, societies, planets, stars, and galaxies. But there are some facts about the world that you could not observe, no matter how big your research budget was. You could only see how the world *is*, not how it *could have been* or *had to be*. That is, you could not observe *possibilities* and *necessities*.

Possibilities are things that could have happened, even if they didn't actually happen. Suppose you and your scientists come across a gambler throwing dice. Suppose the gambler throws double sixes. The dice *could have* come up double ones instead. (Or a one and a two, or any other combination.) *In actuality*, double ones did not occur, but they could have. There are many alternatives to actuality, big and small. In actuality, Germany lost the Second World War, but things might have turned out otherwise. In an alternate possible history, Germany wins. In actuality, there are no unicorns, or 10-feet-tall humans, but there could have been, had history unfolded differently.

Not everything is possible. Unlike unicorns and 10-feet-tall humans, round squares and married bachelors are impossible. In no alternate history are there round squares or married bachelors. Squares *must* be non-round; bachelors *must* be unmarried. Things that must occur are called **necessities**. If you drop a stone, it necessarily falls. If a number is even, it necessarily is divisible by two.

Since you and your scientists only observe what actually happens, you will never observe what might have occurred. In a sense you *will* observe necessities, since things that must happen *do* happen. But you won't observe *that they are necessary*, only that they are actual. David Hume, the Scottish philosopher, pointed this out in the eighteenth century. Let go of a stone and you will see it fall, but you won't see the *necessity* of its falling; you won't see that it *must* fall. Drop stones again and again, and you will see them fall each time, but you will never observe anything more than a regularity—a repeating pattern.

Possibility and necessity are related. To say that something is possible is to say that its failure to happen is not necessary. Unicorns are possible because it is not necessary that they fail to exist. To say that something is necessary is to say that its failure to happen is not possible. It is necessary that all bachelors are unmarried because married bachelors are not possible. Musts and mights are really two sides of the same coin.

Necessity and possibility are philosophically perplexing. For one thing, if we never *observe* mights and musts, how can we *know* about them? This is one of the problems discussed in the branch of philosophy known as **epistemology**, the theory of knowledge. Even sticking to metaphysics, necessity and possibility give us plenty to puzzle over. When something must or might occur, what sort of fact is that? An actual event, for instance, the falling of a stone, is easy to understand. The world contains various objects in time and space, such as stones. And certain events involving those objects occur: stones fall. But what kinds of facts are possibilities? In addition to the actual events we observe, is there also a realm of ghostly unobserved possible events and objects, ghostly dice coming up double ones, ghostly German military victories, ghostly unicorns and 10-feet-tall humans? It is hard to believe that these ghostly entities exist. (And even if they do, why would they count as *possibilities*? Rather than making it the case that *unicorns are possible*, the existence of a ghostly unicorn would just mean that *ghostly things are actual*.) On the other hand, if possibilities are not ghostly entities, what are they?

Necessity, too, is perplexing. Necessary things are things that *must* happen. 'Must' suggests *rules*. But who made these rules, and who enforces them? On the other hand, if the rules picture is wrong, what is mustness? Consider the true sentence 'All bachelors are unmarried'. It is easy to see why this sentence is true: it is true because of certain facts about the physical world. The world contains certain objects—bachelors—and each of these bachelors has a certain property—being unmarried. But our sentence doesn't just *happen* to be true. It is necessarily true; bachelors *must* be unmarried. So there must be something over and above the physical world that changes our sentence from a mere truth into a necessary truth, that turns a mere *is* into a *must*. What is that something?

Let's begin by getting a grip on the very tricky words 'possible' and 'necessary' (and the related words, 'might', 'may', 'could', 'must', etc.) These words can be used to mean different things. Sometimes 'possible' concerns our *knowledge* of the world rather than the world itself. I once asked a friend: 'Have the Montreal Expos ever won the World Series?', and he replied: 'It's possible; I'm not a football fan.' My friend's reply was simply intended to convey his state of ignorance: he did not know whether the Expos had ever won. (His reply conveyed more ignorance than he intended.) These *epistemic* mights and musts are not particularly perplexing from a metaphysical point of view. They concern human knowledge, a part of the world of actual events. At other times, 'may' and 'must' concern *morality*. To say that you *must not* murder is to say that murder would be morally *wrong*. Unlike epistemic mights and musts, moral mights and musts raise interesting metaphysical issues. Where in the world of actual events can morality be located? Is morality merely a function of society, or does the moral realm transcend human practice? If the latter, what does morality involve?

Fascinating as these epistemic and moral issues are, let us restrict our focus to *metaphysical* uses of 'possible' and 'necessary'. Even then, these tricky words can signify different things. The remainder of this chapter will focus on two metaphysical varieties of possibility and necessity: *natural* and *absolute*.

Natural Possibility and Necessity

Natural possibility and necessity concern the **laws of nature**. When a stone is dropped, it must fall. Burning methane and oxygen must react to produce carbon dioxide and water. Anyone with certain DNA must have blue eyes. The laws of nature governing the physical world—the laws of physics, chemistry, and biology (and perhaps other sciences)—guarantee certain behavior of stones, chemicals, and DNA. These laws say that certain outcomes *must* occur; those outcomes are *naturally necessary.*

Scientists try to discover the laws of nature. That is their job. Physicists seek the laws of physics; chemists, the laws of chemistry; biologists, the laws of biology. Learning the laws has a practical side: understanding nature gives us more control over it, and over our lives. But it also has a purely intellectual side. If you could interview God and ask her the truth about the world, you would not want her merely to list all the events that actually happened. You would also want to know *why* certain events followed other events, what *principles* govern the unfolding of history.

By 'laws of nature' I mean the *real* laws of nature, as opposed to what scientists believe the laws to be at any given time. Scientists once thought the laws of physics allowed travel in excess of the speed of light. That was just a mistake (though a perfectly understandable mistake at the time). Superluminal travel is, and has always been, prohibited by the laws of nature (assuming today's physicists have got it right!).

Just what *is* a law of nature? Don't take the word 'law' too seriously. Laws of nature are nothing like the laws we institute to govern society. A few people break society's laws, but nothing ever breaks the laws of nature; no renegade stones fly up in the air when dropped, just out of spite. Also, unlike society's laws, the laws of nature have no legislators. No person or persons legislated the rule that dropped stones fall. It's not as if each stone has a little rulebook it consults. 'OK, I've been dropped; what must I do? Let's see, *Code of Behavior for Stones*, page 39, paragraph B. Yes, here it is: "when dropped, fall!". Ok, then, here goes!' That's silly.

Or is it? One might reply that laws of nature *are* legislated: by God. This theory of laws makes a big presupposition: that God exists. But even granting this presupposition, the divine legislation theory is problematic, for God legislates many things that aren't laws of nature. Suppose there is now an odd number of trees in North America. That is not naturally necessary; no law of nature insures it. It just turned out that way. But if there is a God, the number of trees in North America is just as much under her control as anything else. So we cannot define a law of nature as something legislated by God. When God created the world, she must have done something extra when she said LET DROPPED STONES FALL, as opposed to when she said LET THE NUMBER OF TREES IN NORTH AMERICA IN 2005 BE ODD. She must have done something extra to make the first, but not the second, a law of nature. And the divine theory gives us no clue as to what that something extra is.

A better theory is the **regularity theory**, according to which a law of nature is nothing more than a *regularity*, that is, a pattern in the world that holds at all times and places. It is a law of nature that dropped stones fall, simply because all dropped stones (here and everywhere, past, present and future) in fact fall. Nothing more is required, because that's all a law is—a regularity.

The regularity theory has one very big thing going for it: it demystifies laws. No little rulebooks, or legislating God, are required to explain laws, if laws are just patterns in the events that actually occur. Recall you and your scientists observing the world. If the regularity theory is true, you really could observe the laws of nature, if you had genuinely unlimited time and resources and so could observe all times and places.

But the regularity theory conflicts, in a number of ways, with our ordinary conception of laws. First, saying that laws are just regularities seems to leave out the *necessity* of laws. How can a regular pattern of dropped stones falling, however uniform and long-lasting, make it true that a dropped stone *must* fall?

Second, consider the regularity that all dropped stones fall. *Why* do dropped stones always fall? What is the *explanation*? According to our ordinary conception, the regularity holds *because* of the law that dropped stones must fall. The law *makes* the regularity true. But if the law just *is* the regularity, the law can neither explain the regularity nor make it true.

Third, the regularity theory makes laws of nature too *global*. It says that a law is spread out over all of space and time, since a law is just an overarching pattern. We ordinarily think that natural necessity is more *local* than that. When a dropped stone falls, the fact that it must fall concerns only the stone and the surrounding circumstances, not the totality of stones throughout all of space and time.

These three problems show how the regularity theory conflicts with our ordinary conception of laws of nature. The defender of the regularity theory might respond by flatly rejecting our ordinary conception. Perhaps that conception comes from a mistaken picture of laws of nature as being like laws of society, or like little rulebooks that stones and other physical objects carry around with them for guidance.

But there is a devastating fourth problem with the regularity theory: some regularities are clearly *not* laws of nature. Here are two examples. First: let N be the maximum number of people that ever attend a single dinner party on a Thursday evening. Then the following is a regularity: *every dinner party on a Thursday is attended by N or fewer people.* If the regularity theory is true, then it is a law of nature that every dinner party on a Thursday is attended by N or fewer people. But that is obviously wrong. Suppose N is 15. It is obviously just *happenstance* that no more than 15 people ever attend a Thursday dinner party. No law of nature prohibits 16 people from attending a Thursday dinner party; larger dinner parties might easily have occurred. Regularities like this are just *coincidental.* Second example: suppose that I weigh exactly 160.35714 pounds, am exactly 68.56865 inches tall, and no one else in the past, present, or future is exactly that height and weight. (If by a miracle there is, surely this other person does not also have red birthmarks on his or her right index and middle fingers, as I do. We could then add information about these birthmarks to the height and weight, thus achieving a characteristic that is unique to me.) Let me tell you one more thing about myself: my favorite move in basketball is the jump shot. (Fake to the right, crossover dribble to the left, pull up for the shot. Swish, every time.) So, here is a regularity: *every person who weighs exactly 160.35714 pounds and is exactly 68.56865 inches tall has the jump shot as his favorite basketball move.* Since I am the only person in all of history with this exact height and weight, it is true that *everyone* in history with that height and weight likes this move. Yet it is obvious that, even though this is an exceptionless regularity, it is no law of nature. My liking the jump shot has nothing to do with my height and weight. I could just as easily have preferred the no-look pass instead.

Defenders of the regularity theory can try to revise their theory so as not to count just any regularity as a law. But instead of tinkering, let us consider a very different sort of theory. According to the **universals theory**, laws of nature arise from connections between universals.[1] First, what are universals? A universal is what is common to similar things. The universal *white*, for example, is what is shared by all white things; the universal *1 gram mass* is shared by anything that has 1 gram mass. The various *instances* of *white* are all the different objects that are white—white pieces of paper, white shirts, and so on. The universal *white* is a single entity that is common to all these instances.

Now for the universals theory of laws. Consider the following chemical law: methane and oxygen must react to produce carbon dioxide and water. Intuitively, this law is more than just the regularity that methane and oxygen always do react to produce carbon dioxide and water. The universals theorist locates the extra bit in a fact about the universals *methane, oxygen, carbon dioxide*, and *water*: these universals are related to one another in such a way that any instances of the first two react to produce instances of the second two. In short: the universals *methane* and *oxygen* **necessitate** the universals *carbon dioxide* and *water*.

This theory avoids the four troubles afflicting the regularity theory. Even though it is a regularity that every person who weighs exactly 160.35714 pounds and is exactly 68.56865 inches tall likes shooting jump shots, the universals theorist can say that this is not a law, since the universals *weighing 160.35714 pounds* and *measuring 68.56865 inches* do not necessitate the universal *liking the jump shot*. Regularities do not imply necessitations. So not all regularities turn out to be laws. That's good; the fourth problem for the regularity theory is solved by the universals theory. It's

[1] Chapter 8 discusses many issues about universals, including some of the assumptions about universals that are made by the universals theory of laws.

also good that laws turn out to be local rather than global. According to the universals theory, a law is a fact about the universals involved, not about all of time and space. When methane and oxygen combine to produce carbon dioxide and water at a certain place and time, the universals *methane* and *oxygen* are located then and there, and necessitate the universals *carbon dioxide* and *water*, which are also located then and there. No other places or times are involved. Third problem solved. And it's good that the universals theorist's laws can explain regularities. Unlike the regularity theory, the universals theory does not say that laws and regularities are the same thing. And while regularities do not imply necessitations, necessitations (i.e. laws) *do* imply regularities. If universal U necessitates universal V, then all Us must be Vs. So the universals theorist can say that U's necessitating V *explains* the regularity that all Us are Vs, thus solving the second problem. Finally, since the universals theorist's laws are not mere regularities, they seem intuitively to be more necessary than the laws of the regularity theorist. The first problem is solved too.

But remember the whole point of the regularity theory: to demystify laws. The universals theory takes a big step backward here. For the concept of necessitation is a mystery. What does it mean to say that *methane* and *oxygen* 'necessitate' *carbon dioxide* and *water*? Do these universals carry little rulebooks? Here is how I described the necessitation between *methane, oxygen, carbon dioxide*, and *water* earlier: 'these universals are related to each other in such a way that any instances of the first two react to produce instances of the second two'. This may have superficially appeared to be a good explanation, but in fact it is not. It just restates the fact we want to explain: the fact that methane and oxygen react to produce carbon dioxide and water. It does nothing to answer the question we are asking: what specifically about the relationship between these universals produces the regularity? An associate once gave me a similar pseudo-explanation. When I asked him how a silencer gun works, his answer was that 'the gun is constructed so that the sound waves don't escape'.

The question of laws of nature is a difficult one. Turning laws into regularities demystifies them by making them part of the ordinary world of events; on the other hand, doing so is incompatible with our ordinary conception of laws as local explainers of regularities. It is hard to know what to think.

Absolute Possibility and Necessity

On that uncertain note, let us turn now to our second metaphysical variety of possibility and necessity: **absolute** possibility and necessity. Recall two of our initial examples of necessities: if you let go of a stone, it must fall; and, any bachelor must be unmarried. These two examples are actually very different from each other. In addition to pointing out that necessity cannot be observed, David Hume also pointed out that exceptions to laws of nature are imaginable. It is easy to imagine a dropped stone hovering in mid-air, or levitating, or turning into Barry Manilow. But try as you might, you cannot imagine a married bachelor, since bachelors by definition are unmarried. The fact that bachelors are unmarried is necessary in a much stronger sense than the fact that dropped stones fall.

We can imagine worlds in which dropped objects turn pink, methane and oxygen combine to produce Gatorade, and eye color is determined by your date of birth. None of these events are *naturally* possible, since they violate the actual laws of nature. But in another sense they *are* possible, for the laws of nature themselves could have been different. These events are *absolutely* possible.

Absolute possibility is the broadest sense of the word 'possible'. Unicorns, flying pigs, and violations of the laws of nature are all absolutely possible. What is *not* absolutely possible? The clearest cases are contradictions in terms: a married bachelor, a round square, a person who is taller than himself, a day in which it both rains and never rains, an empty box with something in it.

Absolute possibility is the broadest sort of possibility, which means that it is very *easy* for something to be absolutely possible. Even violations of the laws of nature are absolutely possible, for example. The flip side of this is that absolute necessity is the *narrowest* sort of necessity; in other words, it is very *hard* for something to be absolutely necessary. Lots of things that are naturally necessary are not absolutely necessary, like stones falling when dropped. The only things that are absolutely necessary are things whose falsity is not absolutely possible. It is absolutely necessary that all bachelors are unmarried, and that it is raining if it is raining.

Absolute necessity and possibility are integral to philosophy itself. One of philosophy's distinctive features is that it investigates **essences**. And the essence of something is what is absolutely necessarily true of it. In ethics one seeks the essence of right and wrong; one seeks a theory of *what it is* to be right and wrong. That means finding a theory of right and wrong that is absolutely necessarily true. It is not enough to find a useful guide to right and wrong, a guide that is right most of the time. For if the guide ever delivers the wrong recommendation—if it is even absolutely *possible* for it to deliver the wrong recommendation—then it cannot capture the essence of right and wrong, and so is an unacceptable philosophical theory. Another example: in our study of personal identity, we sought to uncover the essence of personal identity—of continuing to exist over time. To succeed, we needed an account that was necessarily true. That was why it was appropriate to dream up thought experiments in which memories were swapped by evil scientists. Even if these exotic events never actually occur, they *might* have occurred in certain exotic circumstances. A good theory of the essence of personal identity should still correctly apply in those circumstances. If the spatiotemporal continuity theory is to be true, it must be absolutely necessary that a person persists over time if and only if that person retains spatiotemporal continuity.

Given the breadth of absolute possibility, the need for demystification is particularly acute. Nobody believes that the many and varied absolute possibilities float, in ghostly form, throughout our humdrum world of space and time! So: what are absolute possibilities?

One exciting idea is that they are **possible worlds**. Let's imagine a few possible worlds. World one: a world in which history went much as it actually did, but in which the Germans won the Second World War. World two: a world in which there exists nothing but a single rock, all alone, just sitting there, for all of eternity. World three: a world much like ours, except that every five days, at midnight EST, everyone on earth joins together and sings Barry Manilow's 'Copacabana'. World four: a world in which gravity works in reverse, so that massive objects repel rather than attract each other. In short, every complete alternative history that could have occurred is a possible world. The only things *not* contained in possible worlds are round squares, married bachelors, and the like—absolutely impossible things.

Flying pigs and planetwide songs are obviously absent from the physical world we experience. But according to the twentieth-century American philosopher David Lewis, they exist nonetheless: in other possible worlds. Figure 11 is a picture of reality according to David Lewis. The circles represent different possible worlds. These other possible worlds are not like distant planets. Mercury, Venus, Mars and the rest are all in *our* possible world. Possible worlds are entirely separated from one another: each has its own space and time and its own objects (so you can't travel to another one—sorry). Our world, the actual world, is just one world among many. The others are just as real as ours.

ACTUAL WORLD   **OTHER POSSIBLE WORLDS**

Fig. 11. David Lewis's actual and possible worlds

A Lewisian possible world is a separate, self-contained realm of space and time.

Given Lewis's possible worlds, we can define absolute possibility and necessity. Something is absolutely necessary if it is true in *every* possible world; something is absolutely possible if it is true in *some* possible world.

The best thing about Lewis's theory is that it thoroughly demystifies absolute necessity and possibility. Lewis has no use for ghostly possibilities. He first confines flying pigs and other possibilities to their own possible worlds, so that they do not infest ours; then he removes their ghostly status by claiming that they are just as real as the objects in our world. Possible flying pigs are just as real and non-ghostly as our own actual pigs; the only difference is that they are *there* (in their possible world) and our pigs are *here*.

But the price is believing in flying pigs, planet-wide Copacabanas, and massive bodies that repel each other! In general it is irrational to believe in things without positive reason to do so. That is why adults don't believe in the tooth fairy or Santa Claus. So we should reject Lewis's worlds unless he gives us reasons to believe in them.

In fact, Lewis says that we *do* have a reason to believe in his possible worlds: only by believing in them can we demystify necessity and possibility. I personally find it hard to bring myself to believe in flying pigs for such a theoretical reason. Still, Lewis has a point: it *is* sometimes reasonable to postulate things for theoretical reasons. In a sense, no one has ever directly perceived an electron. Physicists postulate electrons to explain the results of the experiments they perform. But demystifying necessity and possibility may not be a strong enough reason to believe in Lewis's worlds.

The issue would be moot if one could demystify possibility and necessity without postulating Lewis's worlds. **Conventionalism** is an alternative theory of necessity and possibility that attempts to do just that. Conventionalism says that all absolute necessities are *true by definition*. Speakers of the English language have instituted a convention of using the word 'bachelors' for unmarried men. It follows from this convention that 'all bachelors are unmarried' is true. It similarly follows from the meanings we give to the words 'taller than', 'either ... or', and 'not' that the sentences 'no one is taller than himself' and 'it is either raining or it is not raining' are true. According to conventionalism, something is absolutely necessary if it is true by definition; and something is absolutely possible if is not true by definition that it is false. (Conventionalism is only intended as a theory of absolute necessity, not of natural necessity. The laws of nature are obviously not true by definition!)

Conventionalism demystifies possibility and necessity in a big way, by turning necessity and possibility into a matter of definitions. How we define words is clearly part of the natural world. No possible worlds or ghostly possibilities needed!

But are all necessities really true by definition? Here is a problematic case. Consider Bill Clinton. Clinton might have been different in many ways. Had things turned out otherwise, he might never have been impeached. In fact, he might never have been president; he might have lost the 1992 election, or even never entered politics. He might have been much shorter, or taller. He might have lived in a different country. He might have had electric blue hair. But now: could he have been a *flower*? We can of course imagine an eccentric person naming a flower 'Bill

Clinton'. But the question is not whether a flower could have been *named* 'Bill Clinton'. The question is whether a flower could have *been* Bill Clinton. Concerning the man actually called Bill Clinton (i.e. the actual 42nd president of the United States), could *he* have been a flower? And the answer seems to be no. There are limits on the kinds of changes we can imagine to an entity while having it still count as the same entity. Whereas we can imagine Clinton being taller, living in a different country, or having a different profession, we cannot imagine him being a flower. Any flower would not be *him*. Likewise, it seems that Clinton could not have been a table, or an antelope.[2] In short, Clinton could not have been anything other than a human being. That is, it is an absolutely necessary truth that Bill Clinton is a human being. But the sentence 'Bill Clinton is a human being' does *not* seem to be true by definition, for unlike the word 'bachelor', which carries a definition (unmarried male), the name 'Bill Clinton' has no definition. It just stands for Bill Clinton. We all *know* that Bill Clinton is a human being, but this isn't built into the meaning of the name 'Bill Clinton' by definition.

A second problematic case for conventionalism involves philosophical inquiry. As we noted earlier, philosophy investigates the essences of concepts, and thus investigates what is absolutely necessary. Ethicists seek the essence of right and wrong. Aestheticians seek the essence of beauty. Epistemologists seek the essence of knowledge. Metaphysicians seek the essences of personal identity, free will, time, and so on. According to conventionalism, these investigations ultimately concern definitions. It seems to follow that one could settle any philosophical dispute just by consulting a dictionary! Anyone with experience with philosophy knows it is never that easy.

---

[2] These limits on *possible* changes are somewhat like the limits discussed in Chapter 1 on what changes *over time* a person can undergo and still remain the same person.

Conventionalists may respond by adopting a new definition of 'true by definition', one not tied to dictionaries. After all, dictionaries are not the sources of meanings; they record pre-existing patterns of word-use. Evaluating this response could take an entire book on its own. There is a lot at stake here, and not just the status of necessity. If conventionalism is true, philosophy turns into nothing more than an inquiry into the definitions we humans give to words. By demystifying necessity, the conventionalist demystifies philosophy itself. Conventionalists are typically up front about this: they *want* to reduce the significance of philosophy. But their picture of philosophy is a far cry from its traditional aspirations.

FURTHER READING

Here are two books that discuss laws of nature. David Hume's book, especially section VII, defends a regularity theory, and is the classic source of the problem of laws of nature (and the related problem of the nature of causality). David Armstrong's book criticizes the regularity theory of laws, defends the universals theory, and is generally very readable.

David Hume, *An Enquiry Concerning Human Understanding* (1748).
David Armstrong, *What is a Law of Nature?* (Cambridge University Press, 1983).

Here are two books that discuss absolute necessity. A. J. Ayer's book, especially chapter 4, defends conventionalism. David Lewis's book defends the possible worlds theory of possibility and necessity. Though rich and fascinating, it is difficult and technical.

A. J. Ayer, *Language, Truth and Logic*, 2nd edn. (Dover, 1952).
David Lewis, *On the Plurality of Worlds* (Blackwell, 1986).

CHAPTER 10

What is Metaphysics?

Earl Conee

Introduction

Biology is about life and art history is about the history of art. Likewise, metaphysics is about metaphysics. But what's that? Can we identify the subject matter in some more informative way? In the previous chapters we have considered nine main metaphysical topics and numerous related metaphysical issues. What makes these *metaphysical* topics and issues? Let's consider some candidate answers.

Being qua Being

One answer derives from Aristotle's *Metaphysics*. In that book there is a field of inquiry that Aristotle calls 'first philosophy'. This field seems similar to our metaphysics. Aristotle tells us that first philosophy is the science of being qua being. Is that metaphysics?

Well, first we have to figure out what is meant by 'the science of being qua being'. To begin with, the term 'science' here means theoretical knowledge. Counting anything as metaphysical *knowledge* is optimistic. As we've seen, controversy reigns in metaphysics. Established conclusions are quite rare (at best!). Fortunately, this optimism about knowledge is harmless for our purpose. We may have to gain metaphysical knowledge in order to *complete* a metaphysical inquiry. But we do not now seek to identify what it is to complete a metaphysical inquiry. We seek only to identify the distinctive *subject matter* of metaphysics. Whether or not we have knowledge of any metaphysical facts, we are now just asking what makes some facts metaphysical ones.

As it addresses this question of subject matter, our initial answer from Aristotle gives us the phrase, 'being qua being'. Here is one interpretation of that. The first 'being' in the phrase identifies the topic as existence. The 'qua being' in the phrase adds that the focus of metaphysics is existence in general. It is not about the existence of fish, or the existence of things in the twenty-first century. It is about the general nature of existence. So if Aristotle's 'first philosophy' is metaphysics, then we have the proposal that the subject matter of metaphysics is existence itself. Metaphysics is not about any of the things that exist, or their existence under certain limited conditions. It is purely about existence.

The nature of existence is definitely a metaphysical topic, and a tough one at that. It is challenging to say anything informative about what it is to exist. One metaphysical controversy about existence concerns whether or not existence is a property. To see what is at issue, imagine a balloon that does not exist. Just imagine any merely possible balloon you like. Done? Okay, now imagine that same balloon, but try to add existence to the properties that you are imagining the balloon to have. What did you add? Nothing! Existence does not seem to be a separate property that can be added or deleted. Noting this, some philosophers are led to conclude that existence is not a property at all. Others think that existence is a special property that is required for having any other properties. Existence was already included in your imagining of a possible balloon, because you had to imagine it as existing to imagine it at all. This is a metaphysical dispute that is about existence itself.

We are considering the claim that existence is the subject matter of metaphysics. We have just looked very briefly at one metaphysical issue that is about existence. But much of metaphysics is not about existence. In effect, we have seen this repeatedly in the previous chapters. For instance, the problem of the nature of time is not focused on existence. When the question is that of whether everything is fated in advance, existence is not the topic. Investigating the nature of free will is not studying existence. The same goes for the nature of physical and absolute necessity. The question of whether universals exist does involve existence. But that question about universals is not focused on existence itself. The question is whether universals exist, leaving unexamined the nature of existence. The same comment applies to the topic of the continued existence of persons. The topic is not existence, but rather the conditions under which the identical person retains existence, whatever existence really is.

Thus, if being qua being is sheer existence, then the subject matter of metaphysics is not limited to being qua being.

First Principles

Let's consider a new idea about what metaphysics is about. In Aristotle's *Metaphysics* he also tells us that the philosophy in that book concerns first principles and causes. The topic of causes seems more suited to the natural sciences. So let's consider the thought that metaphysics concerns just first principles. The first principles account of metaphysics suggests one improvement over our previous idea. The plural 'principles' goes some way toward acknowledging the plurality of metaphysical topics.

As it stands, though, 'first principles' is almost an empty phrase. The principles are 'first' *in what ordering*? There are many first principles. Metaphysical principles are surely not the first principles *in a code of ethics for real estate agents*! Likely the idea is that metaphysical principles are 'first' because they are somehow *most basic*. Okay, but now we have to ask: most basic *in what way*? 'Basic' sometimes means elementary. But of course the most elementary principles of accounting are not metaphysics. 'Basic' sometimes means important. But of course the most important principles of fire prevention are not metaphysics. Soon we'll consider a third way in which the topics of metaphysics might be most basic. But no matter what being 'basic' amounts to, we need additional help concerning the principles involved. What are the relevant principles *about*? The phrase 'first principles' does not really specify a subject matter at all.

Appearances vs Ultimate Reality

Let's try a different thought. Metaphysical investigations begin with initial appearances. For instance, one of the metaphysical issues that we have considered begins with the appearance that we act freely sometimes; another of our issues begins with the appearance that there are properties that many things share. Our other topics have their own appearances as starting points. In everyday life, these appearances are seldom questioned. In metaphysics, we investigate further. As we pursue a metaphysical topic, we seek to get beyond appearances. We consider arguments about how things really are. We seek to learn the reality of the situation. Reality may confirm initial appearances or it may undercut them. Either way, our goal is to find the ultimate reality. This suggests that the subject matter distinctive of metaphysics is ultimate reality.

There is something definitely right in this suggestion. The metaphysical facts about freedom, properties, and so on do consist in how things ultimately stand concerning these topics. The appearances are not conclusive. Only the ultimate realities give us the metaphysical truths of the matter.

We should think carefully about the idea of 'ultimate reality'. Suppose that something is real. Its existence is genuine and not a false appearance. Could anything be 'more real' than that, so as to be 'ultimately' real? How? Some things are more important than others in some ways, but that doesn't enhance their reality. When we see things in this light, it looks as though the 'ultimate' in 'ultimate reality' doesn't add anything. Everything actual is as real as things get.

If ultimate reality just consists in the things that actually exist, though, then an orientation toward ultimate reality does not distinguish metaphysics from any other factual investigation. In paleontology, for instance, the apparent nature of apparent fossils is not conclusive. Only the actual nature of actual fossils supply the paleontological truths of the matter. The same goes for police detective work. The apparent facts about a crime are not the end of a criminal investigation. Only when the actual facts of the crime are detected is the detective work truly done. Thus, metaphysics is not distinctively about ultimate reality.

Ultimate Explanations

The appearance/reality distinction may be leading us astray. There is another way to understand what is 'ultimate' about the subject matter of metaphysics. Another idea is that the aspects of reality that metaphysics is about are the 'ultimate' ones in that they are *most fundamental in explanations*.

This idea has a lot going for it. For one thing, the topics discussed in this book all seem to qualify as metaphysical ones by this standard. The questions why anything at all exists, whether or not everything is fated in advance, what physical and absolute necessity really are, whether or not universals exist, whether or not God exists, these all seem to concern facts that are somehow fundamental to explaining reality. The same goes for the nature of freedom, personal identity, material constitution, and time. In contrast, fossils and crimes seem more localized, less basic to explanations.

But metaphysics might not be completely alone in studying the fundamental explanatory realities. What about physics? Doesn't physics investigate elementary constituents of reality and how they account for all physical events and conditions? That sort of explanation seems pretty fundamental.

One reply in defense of the explanatory basics view of metaphysics reminds us about sharing. The reply says that a topic is not excluded from metaphysics just because the topic is also studied in another field. In this view, physics does include inquiry into the metaphysical topic of the elementary constitution of reality. This question is part of physics when it is pursued scientifically. But it remains a metaphysical subject too.

This defense of the proposal that metaphysics is about the most fundamental explanations is itself questionable, though. Physicists often wish to distance their work from metaphysics. They say that they are doing empirical science *rather than* metaphysics. Are they really doing both? Not necessarily. Maybe physicists are not *doing* metaphysics, because they are using scientific methods rather than philosophical ones. But they are scientifically investigating a *subject matter* that they share with metaphysicians.

So we have a promising proposal, although a question about its correctness arises from the overlap with physics. We'll look next at a revised version that avoids any such trouble. It turns out to be promising, but we'll soon see that both versions confront a harder problem.

Basic Necessities and Possibilities

The revised view is that metaphysics is about *the most explanatorily basic necessities and possibilities*. Metaphysics is about what *could* be and what *must* be. Except incidentally, metaphysics is not about explanatorily ultimate aspects of reality that are actual, but need not have existed. Metaphysics is about some actual things, only because whatever is necessary has got to be actual and whatever is possible might happen to be actual. This allows us to say that physics pursues the question of what the basic constitution of reality *actually* is, while metaphysics is about what it *must be* and what it *could have been*.

This new view may allow metaphysics to have exclusive claim to its topics. The view has its own liabilities, however. It seems to leave out much that goes on in the name of metaphysics. For instance, there is the question of whether or not we actually have free will. Answering this question seems as much part of metaphysics as answering the questions of what free will must be and what it might have been. Similarly, the question of why there actually is something rather than nothing seems to be about a contingent fact. Yet this question is as metaphysical as anything is.

These liabilities of the new view may turn out to be illusory. Perhaps the apparently excluded metaphysics does qualify by the present standard, because it turns out to be about possibilities and necessities after all. A metaphysician who seems to be investigating whether we actually have free will may not really be doing just that. Perhaps she is really investigating whether free will is possible for beings such as we are. Similarly, when metaphysicians consider the question of why there is something rather than nothing, maybe they are really seeking some possible explanation for the existence of contingent things. Of course, we are also interested in the actual facts about freedom, contingent things, and so forth. But maybe that important further aspect of our interest technically goes beyond pure metaphysics.

A different problem stems from the phrase 'most explanatorily basic'. The philosophical study of ethics is partly about the nature of morally right conduct. Many philosophers think about this as an inquiry into the nature of the property of being morally right. They regard this issue as squarely in ethics, not metaphysics. Yet the nature of right action seems as fundamental to explanations as, say, the metaphysical topics of fate and free will.

But maybe that's not too bad of a consequence for the current account. Maybe this is a case of overlapping topics, and the study of the nature of moral rightness is a metaphysical topic within ethics.

The problem seems worse when we consider the findings of logic and mathematics. These formal facts all seem to be necessary truths, and some of them seem quite basic to explanations. For one thing, the logic of an explanation—the connection between an explanatory theory and the facts explained—seems to be the most basic thing about it. The present view makes this connection a metaphysical subject matter. That is doubtful. It seems to belong to logic.

Again, this sort of objection may not be conclusive. Maybe logic and metaphysics share this subject matter. They differ by working on it in different ways.

There is a more difficult problem here, though. Both versions of the explanatory basics idea limit the metaphysical subject matter of math and logic to the parts of these fields that play a basic role in explanations. Yet all of the topics of math and logic seem to be metaphysically on a par. These fields study things such as mathematical objects like numbers and the logical features that make for valid arguments. All such things appear to be worthy subjects of metaphysical interest. Perhaps some of them are of special metaphysical significance because they are infinite or otherwise amazing. In any case, what seems to determine their status as metaphysical topics is their interest as entities in their own right, and not their role in explanations. The current idea about the subject matter of metaphysics says otherwise, and so it is in trouble.

Taking Stock

We have thought about the subject matter of metaphysics. We have discovered nothing conclusive. Ah well, that's philosophy for you. The stubbornly unresolved status of philosophical issues dissatisfies those who prefer to study the cut and dried. Philosophers find the status challenging, enticing, and even comforting (since they are unlikely to be rendered obsolete).

Some Concluding Questions

What have we been investigating in this chapter? In a way, we were explicit about that. We have been investigating the nature of the subject matter of metaphysics. But what sort of a topic is that? In particular, was our topic a metaphysical one?

It is tempting to think that the obvious answer to this question is 'Yes'. But we should note that having as our topic the nature of metaphysical topics does not automatically make us have a metaphysical topic. This can be seen by analogy. Physics is about the physical world. So physics surely has a physical topic. But conceivably physics itself is an immaterial thing, perhaps because it consists in abstract propositions that constitute the theoretical truth about the physical world. If so, then physics is *about* the physical world but not *part* of it.

Thus, if we have the nature of physics itself as the topic of an investigation, then that investigation does not automatically have a physical subject matter. Analogously, our inquiry about metaphysics in this chapter might have a non-metaphysical subject matter. So we should ask: if the topic of our investigation into metaphysical topics really is a metaphysical topic, why is that? And if this topic is not metaphysical, then what sort of topic is it?

Finally, now that we have taken up these questions, what is the nature of our topic now?

FURTHER READING

The best way to learn more about what constitutes metaphysics is to learn more metaphysics. Here are collections of essays on numerous metaphysical issues.

W. R. Carter (ed.), *The Way Things are: Basic Readings in Metaphysics* (McGraw-Hill, 1998).

Michael J. Loux (ed.), *Metaphysics: Contemporary Readings (Routledge, 2001).*

Jaegwon Kim and Ernest Sosa (eds.), *Metaphysics: An Anthology* (Blackwell, 1999).

Peter van Inwagen and Dean Zimmerman (eds.), *Metaphysics: The Big Questions (Blackwell, 1998).*

ACKNOWLEDGMENTS

Philosophy is an ongoing and collaborative project: each new philosopher adds to what has already been done. We thank those philosophers on whose work we have drawn. We also thank those who helped by commenting on our chapters: Frank Arntzenius, Mark Briand, Seymore Feldman, Simon Keller, Alice Koller, Ned Markosian, Cei Maslen, Sarah McGrath, Daniel Nolan, Ron Sider, Brock Sides, Saul Smilansky, Mary Tinti, Gabriel Uzquiano, Brian Weatherson, and anonymous readers. Thanks to Frank Arntzenius and Tamar Gendler for the title. Ted Sider would like to thank Fred Feldman for his lectures on free will in his introductory philosophy course at the University of Massachusetts in 1990, which were an enormous help with Chapter 6, and would like to especially thank Eliza Block, Tamar Gendler, and Jill North for their extensive comments on his chapters.

INDEX OF TERMS
AND ABBREVIATIONS

Agent causation 120
Anthropic explanations 103
Antinomy 136

Cause and effect 115
Cohabitation 146
Concept 78, 94, 177
Conceptualism 177
Conclusion 64
Constitution 135
Contingent 103
Continuity
    Nonbranching 18
    Psychological 15
    Spatiotemporal 12
Continuous series 12
Conventionalism 194

Desires, first-order vs. second-
        order 131
Determinism 23, 113
    Hard 117
    Soft 125

Epistemology 157, 182
Essence 191
Essential nature 99

Exists 65
Existing Greatest Conceivable
        Being (EGCB) 80

Four-dimensionalism 147
Free will 112

God 64
Greatest Conceivable Being
        (GCB) 79

Hypertime 46

Infinity 65
Inpiece, outpiece 141
Instantiate 163

Just-matter theory 137

Law of nature 184
Law of the Excluded Middle
        (LEM) 27
Libertarianism 118

Matter, quantities/pieces of 134
Maximally Orderly Huge
        Universe (MOHU) 72

Metaphysical Fatalism 22

Necessary beings 91
Necessitarianism 92
Necessitation 188
Necessity 182
   Absolute 190
   Epistemic 183
   Moral 184
   Natural 184
Nihilism 143
Nominalism 174

Ontological dependence 68
Ontological independence 68
Ontology 62, 154

Particles 143
Personal identity 8
Possibility 181
Possible worlds 192
Premises 64
Principle of Insufficient
   Reason 68
Principle of Sufficient Reason 67
Problem of Evil 86
Property 154
Proposition 31, 102

Q 88
QBB 88
QC 103
QM 89

QWC 104
Quantum mechanics 122

Regularity theory 186
Relations 163

Sameness (Identity)
   Numerical 8
   Qualitative 8
Self-instantiation 165
Sets 172
Singular concept 78
Space-time
   Diagrams 48
   Theory 48
Soul 10
Sparse universalist 169

Takeover theory 139
Target of a singular concept 80
Temporal parts 49, 147
Things 159
Tropes 171

UN 166
Universal 155
Universalist 158
Universals theory (of laws of
   nature) 188

W 89
W* 101